JAPAN AND IMPERIALISM,

1853–1945

Key Issues in Asian Studies, No. 7

AAS Resources for Teaching About Asia

JAPAN AND IMPERIALISM,

1853–1945

JAMES L. HUFFMAN

Association for Asian Studies, Inc.
1021 East Huron Street
Ann Arbor, MI 48104 USA
www.asian-studies.org

KEY ISSUES IN ASIAN STUDIES

A series edited by Lucien Ellington, University of Tennessee at Chattanooga

"Key Issues" booklets complement the Association for Asian Studies' teaching journal, *Education About Asia*—a practical teaching resource for secondary school, college, and university instructors, as well as an invaluable source of information for students, scholars, libraries, and those who have an interest in Asia.

Formed in 1941, the Association for Asian Studies (AAS)—the largest society of its kind, with more than 7,000 members worldwide—is a scholarly, non-political, non-profit professional association open to all persons interested in Asia.

For further information, please visit www.asian-studies.org

For orders or inquiries, please contact:
Association for Asian Studies, Inc.
1021 East Huron Street, Ann Arbor, MI 48104 USA
Tel: (734) 665-2490; Fax: (734) 665-3801
www.asian-studies.org

Library of Congress Cataloging-in-Publication Data

Huffman, James L., 1941–

Japan and imperialism, 1853–1945 / James L. Huffman.
    p. cm. — (Key issues in Asian studies; no. 7)
Includes bibliographical references.

ISBN 978-0-924304-61-3 (pbk. : alk. paper) 1. Japan—Foreign relations—1868–1912. 2. Japan—Foreign relations—1912–1945. 3. Imperialism—History—19th century 4. Imperialism—History—20th century I. Title.

DS882.6.H84 2010
325'.32095209041--dc22

2010028246

To Dave Barry

for his ideas,
for his integrity,
for his friendship

And to Charles and Mary Chatfield,

for modeling—so gently and
so incisively—the path to
international understanding

About "Key Issues in Asian Studies"

Key Issues in Asian Studies (**KIAS**) is a series of booklets engaging major cultural and historical themes in the Asian experience. *KIAS* booklets complement the Association for Asian Studies' teaching journal, *Education About Asia*, and serve as vital educational materials that are both accessible and affordable for classroom use.

KIAS booklets tackle broad subjects or major events in an introductory but compelling style appropriate for survey courses. Although authors of the series have distinguished themselves as scholars as well as teachers, the prose style employed in *KIAS* booklets is accessible for broad audiences. This series is particularly intended for teachers and undergraduates at two- and four-year colleges as well as advanced high school students and secondary school teachers engaged in teaching Asian studies in a comparative framework.

For further information about *Key Issues in Asian Studies* booklets, *Education About Asia*, or the Association for Asian Studies, visit www.asian-studies.org.

Prospective authors interested in *Key Issues in Asian Studies* or *Education About Asia* are encouraged to contact:

> Lucien Ellington
> University of Tennessee at Chattanooga
> Tel: (423) 425-2118
> Fax (423) 425-5441
> E-Mail: Lucien-Ellington@utc.edu
> www.asian-studies.org/EAA

"Key Issues" booklets available from AAS:

> *Japanese Popular Culture and Globalization* by William M. Tsutsui
>
> *Global India circa 100 CE: South Asia in Early World History* by Richard H. Davis
>
> *Caste in India* by Diane Mines
>
> *Understanding East Asia's Economic "Miracles"* by Zhiqun Zhu
>
> *Political Rights in Post-Mao China* by Merle Goldman
>
> *Gender, Sexuality, and Body Politics in Modern Asia* by Michael Peletz

About the Author

James L. Huffman is H. Orth Hirt Professor of History Emeritus at Wittenberg University in Springfield, Ohio. A former journalist, he taught East Asian history for thirty-five years. He is the author of six books on Japanese history, including *Creating a Public: People and Press in Meiji Japan* (University of Hawaii, 1997), *A Yankee in Meiji Japan: The Crusading Journalist Edward H. House* (Rowman and Littlefield, 2003), and *Japan in World History* (Oxford University, 2010), as well as *Modern Japan: A History in Documents* (Oxford, 2004 and second edition, 2011). With his wife Judith, he also has published translations of two Japanese children's books. He currently resides in Chicago, where he is working on a study of the daily lives of Japanese commoners in the early twentieth century.

Editor's Introduction

There is a strong case that Japan's experience with imperialism is unique among the world's peoples. In a little less than one-hundred years, the Japanese first were subjected to Western imperialism and then with astounding rapidity—utilizing Western nations as a model and Europeans and Americans as advisors—transformed their nation into an empire that included newly constructed national traditions and institutions, an impressive industrial sector, and a powerful military. By the early twentieth century, Japan had acquired colonies, and by the 1930s the nation had embarked upon a course of action that in part triggered World War II and, for the Japanese, a crushing military defeat in 1945. Japanese experiences with the process and consequences of empire building continue to exert both positive and negative influences upon contemporary Japan's economy, foreign policy, and society. Understanding Japan during this period also offers illumination for all those interested in world history, imperialism and its consequences, and Japanese history.

Jim Huffman does a masterful job of telling this important story at a number of different levels. Huffman, initially a journalist before becoming a teacher and scholar, employs concise and vividly descriptive prose to assist readers to better understand the phenomenon of nineteenth- and early-twentieth-century imperialism and Japan's part in that process. Jim strikes a nifty balance between the general narrative and the personal with his succinct, yet convincing accounts of the lives of actual people who shaped and reacted to related events around them. The Japan that emerges in the story is a nation whose leaders, in responding to unprecedented new external challenges, re-conceptualized Japan's role in Asia and in the world.

I am most grateful for the privilege of working with Jim Huffman. Jim, along with Peter Frost, first proposed the idea of a *Key Issues in Asian Studies* series to AAS. Furthermore, in addition to his many other publications throughout the past decade, Jim has written several stellar articles on Japanese history for the AAS teaching journal, *Education About Asia*.

When considering likely authors for *Key Issues* booklets, there was no question in my mind that Jim would do a fine job on this topic and he exceeded my expectations. Thanks also go to John Tucker, John Sagers, and Taylor Atkins who reviewed this manuscript at various stages in its development. I am also deeply grateful to the AAS Editorial Board and Martha Selby in particular, and to AAS Publications Manager, Jonathan Wilson, and AAS Publications Coordinator, Gudrun Patton, for their strong support of pedagogical scholarship projects such as *Key Issues in Asian Studies* and *Education About Asia*.

Lucien Ellington
Series Editor, Key Issues in Asian Studies

Acknowledgments

Although I may have put the words of this booklet to paper, the ideas and inspiration came from more people than I possibly can acknowledge. I feel deeply my debt to a host of women and men who have done the scholarship on which these words and analyses are based. I also owe thanks to ever so many colleagues and friends across the years whose conversations and examples have shaped my thinking about imperialism: among them, Wesley Babian, the late Jackson Bailey, Charles and Mary Chatfield, Pamela Crossley, Ron Edsforth, Dennis Frost, the late Richard Gray, Roger Hackett, Sally Hastings, Marie Kim, Ed Miller, Lou Perez, Patricia Sippel, and Bill Steele.

Then there are those who have edited, evaluated, and worked directly on this booklet. Steve Ericson's gracious, meticulous reading saved me from several errors, both factual and stylistic. Bob Rafferty and Taylor Hafley of Wittenberg University were wonderfully helpful with maps and I owe a great deal to Jan Opdyke's skillful copyediting. Lucien Ellington is an amazing editor, not just of this work but of the general *Key Issues* series and *Education About Asia*; his deep humanity and organizational genius inspire me endlessly. Jon Wilson's advice and skills were appreciated more than I'll ever be able to explain to him; so was his friendship (Go, Manchester United!). And I am thankful to the anonymous readers who saved me from many an oversight or mistake.

Finally, James, Nao, Kristen, Dave—and yes, Grace, Simon, and Ryu: my debt to you is deeper than ever could be paid, even by the most *giri*-conscious Japanese villager. You've lived through so much with me. And you've made me proud. *Thanks!*

CONTENTS

LIST OF MAPS

Japan and Imperialism: A Timeline

Early 1800s	Foreign incursions into Japanese ports
1853	Matthew Perry arrives in Edo Bay, seeks opening of Japan
1854	Treaty of Kanagawa opens ports to American ships
Late 1850s	Antiforeign movements oppose Tokugawa regime
1863–64	European/American attacks on Satsuma and Chōshū domains
1860	First diplomatic embassy to the United States
1862	First diplomatic embassy to Europe
1868	Meiji Restoration topples Tokugawa government
1869	Ezo renamed Hokkaidō, placed under Hokkaidō Colonization Office
1871–73	Iwakura Mission tours the West
1872	Japan frees Chinese laborers aboard Peruvian bark *Maria Luz*
1874	Expedition to Taiwan following Taiwanese murder of Ryūkyū fishermen
1875	Kuril Islands secured under treaty with Russia
1876	Bonin Islands annexed; commercial relations with Korea begin
1879	Ryūkyū Islands taken, made into Okinawa prefecture
1889	Meiji Constitution makes Japan Asia's first constitutional monarchy
1890	Yamagata Aritomo advocates "line of sovereignty," "line of advantage"
1894	Treaty signed, providing that extraterritoriality would end in 1899
1894–95	Sino-Japanese War victory, followed by Triple Intervention forcing Japan to return Liaodong Peninsula to China
1895	Taiwan becomes Japan's first colony; Korea's Queen Min assassinated
1900	Japanese troops assist in ending China's Boxer Rebellion
1902	Anglo-Japanese Alliance signed
1904–5	Russo-Japanese War; Karafuto becomes a colony; Japan moves into Korea, assumes Russian interests in southern Manchuria
1910	Korea annexed

1911	Japan gains tariff autonomy
1912	Taishō Emperor ascends throne
1914	Japan takes Nan'yō (Micronesian islands); islands mandated to Japan in 1919
1915	"Twenty-one Demands" issued to China
1918	Troops sent to Siberia
1919	March First Incident prompts softer policy in Korea and other colonies
1922	Washington Conference limits Japanese naval spending
1924	America bans immigration from Japan
1925	Japan recognizes Soviet Union
1926	Shōwa Emperor ascends throne
1928	Japan signs antiwar Kellogg-Briand Pact; army extremists assassinate Manchurian warlord Zhang Zuolin
1929	Great Depression begins
1930	London Naval Conference continues limits on Japanese naval spending
1931	Manchurian Incident initiates takeover of Manchuria
1932	Manchukuo formed
1933	Japan leaves League of Nations; Tanggu Truce extends Japan's control into China proper
1936	Anti-Comintern Pact signed with Germany
1937	Marco Polo Bridge Incident triggers China war; Shanghai falls in November; Nanjing Massacre occurs in December
1939	Soviets defeat Japan in Nomonhan
1940	Tripartite Pact signed with Germany and Italy
1941	Neutrality Pact signed with Soviet Union; Japan invades southern Indochina; Pearl Harbor bombing starts World War II in Asia
1942	Japan victorious through May, loses in Midway Battle in June
1943	Japan abandons Guadalcanal; war turns defensive
1944–45	Southeast Asian resistance movements lay groundwork for postwar independence
1945	Okinawa falls; atomic bombs dropped; Japan surrenders; empire dismantled

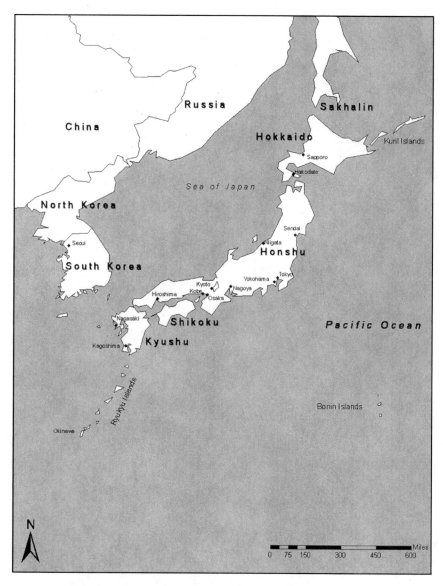

Map 1. Japan Today. (Courtesy of Taylor Hafley.)

INTRODUCTION

I mperialism framed most of Japan's early engagements with the modern
world. A target of European and American expansionism in the mid-
1800s, Japan took a colony of its own in the 1890s and within a generation had
secured a major empire. Choose a page from the imperialist script and Japan
likely experienced it: humiliation by gunboats; impoverishment by unequal
treaties; the exhilaration of military victory; frustrations over colonial costs
and resistance movements; complicated and often brutal interactions with
local peoples.

In this booklet we will examine the story of Japan's encounter with
imperialism from the 1850s, when it was pressured into active engagement
with the Western world, until 1945, when it lost its colonies through war.
The account will draw on both the writings of those involved in the saga and
the analyses of observers, but its focus will be on narrative—on presenting
the events, actors, and trends that made the imperialist experience crucial
to modern history. While we will discuss the interpretations of scholars,
the discussions will occur within the context of the imperialist story. A few
words about the definitions and ideas that have guided its construction should
render that story more understandable.

First, the meaning of *imperialism*. Its classic definition comes from J. A.
Hobson, who described it in 1902 as a system in which the British "annexed
or otherwise asserted political sway over vast portions of Africa and Asia";
he argued that it evolved naturally, but not necessarily, from capitalism.[1]
The Marxist theorist and Russian revolutionary Nikolai Lenin published an
influential economic analysis fourteen years later—*Imperialism, the Highest
State of Capitalism*—which accepted Hobson's description but contended—
incorrectly, most of today's scholars say—that the progression from
capitalism to imperialism was inevitable and that imperialism would, in turn,
cause capitalist states to fall. Others added nuances of their own, with many
discounting capitalism as the primary engine of imperialism. William Langer
contended in the 1930s that imperialism resulted mainly from a desire to
protect (rather than expand) markets; Ronald Robinson and John Gallagher

talked about *informal* imperialism, created by the dynamics of free trade; Carlton Hayes insisted that nationalism, reinforced by Christian missionary movements, fostered the imperialist instinct; and Joseph Schumpeter said its sources were primarily atavistic, springing from the primitive human tendency to fight and dominate. In the early 1980s, a group of Americans— James Thomson Jr., Peter Stanley, and John Perry—added the element of "sentiment," arguing that U.S. imperialism in East Asia had been fueled by a sentimental desire to share "America's sense of distinctiveness," a fact that rendered it no less odious.[2] Examining the debates, it becomes clear that these differences have more to do with causes than definition. Each writer describes a similar basic process: *one nation's assertion of control over another people, either by direct acquisition or by more informal means, usually economic, military, or political.* That will be our working definition.

A related term that will be featured in this study is *colonialism.* While the influential historian Jürgen Osterhammel refers to colonialism as "a phenomenon of colossal vagueness," he demonstrates that it always involves taking control of another people's spaces.[3] If imperialism seeks dominance (either formally or informally), colonialism acquires territory. These two terms are not, however, mutually exclusive; their boundaries are more often vague and overlapping than distinct. When, after all, the Japanese of the early 1900s talked imperialistically about Dai Nihon Teikoku, or "Great Imperial Japan," they usually had colonies in mind. Indeed, the garb that imperialism will most often put on in this story is colonialism.

Even more important than terminology are the concepts that drive this work. First, it seems clear that Japan's imperialist policies—both its responses to Western threats and its actions as a colonizer—grew out of historical contingencies. Leaders may have acted wisely or they may have acted foolishly, but they always were responding to world events as they understood them, not following some overarching plan or unique national characteristic. Japan built a strong military in the late 1800s because its leaders felt threatened by imperialist might; they pursued a conciliatory policy after World War I because global trends were tending that way; and they sought economic self-sufficiency and a stronger empire in the early 1930s because the Great Depression convinced them that they had relied too much on the international economic system. Different people might read the times differently, but they all tried to follow them.

A related assumption is that as an empire builder Japan acted much like the other imperialist powers, not in some "East Asian" way. While fairly standard now, this has not always been the prevailing view. Scholars long have been prone toward what Edward Said refers to as "orientalizing" the Japanese, to talking about their exoticism, their "unique" characteristics, or their "exceptional" historical development. But the study of imperial development makes it clear that Japan followed roughly the same patterns as other empire builders. When the Japanese talked about "bringing civilization" to Korea in the 1890s, they used language similar to the Americans' "white man's burden." And when they exploited colonies economically or imposed authoritarian rules, they acted very much like Great Britain and France in Africa and Asia. A British journalist who suggested that "bullets and bayonets" were "the only trustworthy propagandists of Western Civilization" was describing a gap between the lofty ideals and brutal reality that occurred in West and East alike.[4]

The third contention of this work is that Japanese imperialism (like that of all nations) also had its own distinctive features. These distinctions included the cultural affinity of the Japanese colonizers with their subjects and the fact that most colonies already were well-developed states when Japan took them over. Even more important, as arguably the only imperialist victim to later become a colonial power, Japan came late to the process, taking its first colony in 1895, just as Western imperialism was about to lose its expansive vigor. Japanese colony building also was more strategically driven than that of European nations, particularly in the early years, focused more on meeting national needs than on satisfying business communities. Japan was the sole imperialist power to promote industrialization in its colonies. And unlike any other powers except Russia, Japan colonized only regions within its own geographic zone.

Japan's imperialism also was multicausal, driven by forces and goals as varied as the actors and eras that supported it. There is little question that economic motivations were important, as Japan sought to improve itself through resource development and trade. But they were only part of the story—initially a small part. Forced into the global arena by gunboats, Japan's early modern leaders concluded that prestige and power were essential to security. The initial drive toward empire thus focused on strategic concerns: holding the Westerners at bay, gaining international respect, and satisfying the clamor of domestic critics. Economics became more important later but even then only in tandem with strategic military and domestic concerns.

A final theme is that the imperialist path was evolutionary. If the mid-1800s confronted Japan with the danger of being colonized, the 1870s found it defining its borders, turning peripheral regions such as Hokkaidō in the north and the Ryūkyū Islands to the south into what Tak Matsusaka calls a "no man's-land between empire and nation."[5] Direct empire building began in 1895, with the acquisition of Taiwan after war with China, and for the next two decades Japan took territories aggressively: Karafuto (the southern half of Sakhalin Island, north of Hokkaidō) in 1905, Korea in 1910, and the Micronesian island chains known as Nan'yō in 1914. A less explosive period followed, with relatively quiet expansion into China's northeastern provinces, known as Manchuria. Then, during the Great Depression, the approach changed markedly. Economic self-sufficiency—autarky—became the central goal, administrative practices grew harsher, and Manchuria was turned into a puppet state named Manchukuo. This last shift, in turn, drew Japan more deeply into China and alienated it from its Western allies in a process that ended with World War II. The direction always was outward, but the movement was uneven, based on dynamic, evolving responses to a changing world.

1

THREATENED BY IMPERIALISM
(1853–1868)

E arly in 1863, the dapper young samurai Fukuchi Gen'ichirō returned to
Edo (present-day Tokyo) from a fact-finding mission to Europe, eager
to share a thousand ideas with superiors and colleagues. But "only two or
three friends, besides my wife and an old servant . . . came by to visit," he
recalled in a memoir; everyone "acted as if they didn't know me."[1] A year
later, a group of intellectuals invited him for a discussion of foreign affairs;
at the end of the session, they told him that they had planned to kill him that
day but his comments had convinced them he was a patriot so they would
let him live.

What was Fukuchi's crime? It was nothing more than being infatuated
with Western culture in a xenophobic time. Only a decade earlier, national
policy had barred most foreigners from entering Japan. In the spring of 1854,
however, the government had opened the country in response to American
demands, and each succeeding year had posed fresh challenges: foreigners
demanding new concessions, businessmen disrupting traditional commercial
patterns, regional lords competing for power, antiforeign zealots terrorizing
the streets, and a government trying desperately to hold things together.
Being pro-Western and talkative was dangerous.

To comprehend Fukuchi's dilemma—and the impact of Japan's first
direct encounter with imperialism—requires an understanding of the
midcentury political situation. The administrative center in Edo was headed
by the Tokugawa family, which had presided since 1600 over a structure
called the bakufu ("tent government," a term harking back to an earlier,
military era). Under a system sometimes labeled centralized feudalism, the
Tokugawa held direct control over an eighth of the country's land and ran
such "national" matters as mining, major highways, and foreign affairs, while
250 daimyos (lords) ruled local domains. The glue that held the structure
together was an "alternate attendance" system, under which each daimyo
was required to spend half of his time in Edo, attending the Tokugawa lord,

or shogun, and to leave his wife and children there all the time, as hostages. The daimyo's annual procession to and from Edo, accompanied by up to a thousand sword-bearing retainers, filled the highways with commerce and ceremony. The system had brought Japan two centuries of peace, giving the daimyos considerable autonomy yet assuring their loyalty to the shogun and keeping them strapped for finances.

The bakufu was in trouble when American naval commodore Matthew Perry arrived in 1853, demanding an end to seclusion. Bedeviled by budget shortfalls and paralyzed by both ceremonial rules and bureaucratic infighting, the Tokugawa found themselves under attack from every quarter. But that did not mean Japan was stagnant. The government may have been in crisis, but society was full of energy. Literacy rates ranked among the world's highest thanks to thousands of schools that made education available everywhere. Farming techniques were improving, and agricultural productivity was

Fig. 1.1. Commodore Matthew Perry, who led America's 1853 mission to open Japan, was photographed in this daguerreotype by the famed photographer Matthew Brady. (Courtesy of the U.S. National Archives.)

increasing. Urban cultural life flourished, with pleasure quarters producing wood-block prints, novels, and female entertainment for people of all classes. And a massive print culture had created a sense of nation, with people sharing knowledge, opinions, and commerce along an impressive network of roadways.

The government's crisis was fueled partly by a growing threat from Westerners in the early 1800s. For two hundred years, bakufu officials had maintained order by restricting international intercourse, with Japanese forbidden from traveling abroad and foreigners allowed into Japan only under stringent regulations. Japan's sole Europeans after the 1640s had been a handful of Dutch, who were allowed to trade on the small Nagasaki harbor island of Dejima. Among Asians, the Chinese were restricted to special quarters in Nagasaki, while Koreans and Ryūkyū Islanders came only on diplomatic missions. While officials found ways to stay in touch with world events, they kept foreigners at bay. And they tried to exclude Christianity altogether, convinced that it contained the seeds of rebellion.

Unfortunately for the Tokugawa, developments in the Western hemisphere made the seclusion policy increasingly difficult to enforce after the 1700s. The rise of machine-based manufacturing fueled an Industrial Revolution in Europe, which in its turn prompted Westerners to seek resources and markets around the globe. Ships from Russia, Great Britain, and America began visiting Japanese ports from time to time. And Japan's responses ran the gamut from an 1825 Tokugawa order that visiting ships be expelled immediately to calls by some opinion leaders for engagement with the West. The Confucian pragmatist Honda Toshiaki, representing the latter, recommended trade relations, arguing that Japan should sell rice to "Russia and elsewhere," then buy "goods from other lands such as medicines and valuable manufactures that we do not possess here."[2] One result of the Western incursions was the shattering of the bakufu/daimyo equilibrium.

On the other side of the Pacific, the 1800s saw increasing demands from the American public to force Japan open, with Christian missionaries eager to convert the "heathen," businessmen trumpeting commerce, and the media discussing America's "Manifest Destiny" to spread civilization in Asia. In response, Congress authorized the naval mission that brought Perry and four well-armed ships to the shores of Edo Bay on July 8, 1853. In an act that his interpreter described as "the beginning of American interference in Asia," Perry demanded that Japanese ports be opened to American ships then sailed away, promising to come back the following year.[3] His return in February—this time with eight ships—resulted in the Treaty of Kanagawa, which opened two ports for safety and supplies (but not trade) and provided for American consuls to reside in Japan after 1856. Considerable drinking accompanied the negotiations, and gifts were given by both sides, including silks and porcelains from the Japanese and revolvers and a quarter-scale model train from the Americans. Sailing away, Perry could hardly have known the domestic storm his treaty would set off.

Fig. 1.2. In this American lithograph, members of Matthew Perry's staff are seen giving gifts to the Japanese during their 1853–54 mission to "open" the country. The gifts included a barrel of whiskey, a telegraph instrument, and a model train. (Courtesy of the U.S. National Archives.)

The tumult's first clouds were seeded by the bakufu when it sought advice from the daimyos on how to respond to Perry. While the lords' opinions were too varied to help, the fact of being asked emboldened regional rivals even as it invited activist thinkers into the national debate. On the antiforeign side, hundreds of young *shishi* (high-spirited patriots) trumpeted the slogan "honor the emperor; expel the barbarians" and set out to drive away the Westerners who had followed in Perry's wake. Their main achievement was to create confusion with acts of terrorism: murdering the first American envoy's secretary, burning down the British legation, assassinating high officials, and threatening Fukuchi's life. An even more serious problem for Tokugawa officials was the intensification of antibakufu sentiment within the governing class. By the 1860s, daimyos and activists from several domains had begun using the emperors (who for centuries had resided powerlessly in Kyoto) to challenge the Tokugawa. In 1864, important factions from the western domain of Chōshū went so far as to attempt a military takeover of the court in an effort to establish an anti-Tokugawa power base. They failed, but their assault dramatized how tenuous Tokugawa leadership had become.

The bakufu was not without resources, however; nor was it inactive. Tokugawa officials threw themselves into a two-pronged effort to save the regime and meet the international challenges. Their leaders may not have envisioned the creation of a new order, but they responded to the imperialist intrusion as actively and realistically as probably was possible given the Americans' and Europeans' strength. And the results, while ultimately disastrous for the Tokugawa, were transformative for Japan, laying the groundwork for a new approach to governance and diplomacy that would propel the country to world dominance.

Unfortunately for the Tokugawa, the foreigners who confronted the Japanese now were different from those with whom Japan had dealt in earlier centuries. They made more requests. They were more persistent. They demanded that Japan engage the world with treaties and arms rather than through the ritualized order of traditional East Asia. Operating from a position of material and military strength, the powers negotiated endlessly— for a commercial treaty, additional ports, and the right to spread Christianity. And when Japan resisted, they resorted to arms. In 1863, for example, British ships leveled portions of the southern city of Kagoshima in response to the murder of a British citizen near Yokohama. And in 1864 an expedition of British, French, Dutch, and Americans assaulted Shimonoseki, the capital of Chōshū, officially in retaliation for samurai attacks on Western ships that had entered the harbor (illegally) the previous year but really in an effort to get more treaty ports opened. The Japanese learned from such episodes that imperialists backed their demands with force. In the words of historian Tōyama Shigeki, "There was a real danger that Japan would become a colony."[4]

Despite their military and political weakness, Tokugawa officials equaled the imperialists in savvy and determination. They negotiated fiercely. The first American consul, Townsend Harris, expressed exasperation in his diary over the careful way in which Japanese diplomats debated. "The more I yielded and acquiesced, the more they would impose on me," he wrote on a day when he had "offered them cannon balls for arguments." The Japanese were effective, says diplomatic historian Michael Auslin, because negotiation was a historic part of Japan's governing process. Even the bakufu structure, he says, resembled "a type of international order" in which one had to negotiate with 250 domains to maintain power.[5] Military weakness might force the Japanese to accept unequal treaties, but skill and tenacity prevented the country from being overwhelmed. In signing a commercial treaty with the United States in 1858, for example, Japan had to accept severe tariff restrictions and grant

9

extraterritoriality, which deprived it of legal jurisdiction over Americans living in Japan. But in other instances Japan's diplomats outmaneuvered the foreigners, placing treaty ports in easy to control locations, securing agreements to delay port openings, and manipulating the content of coins to prevent a currency drain.

The Tokugawa also took the initiative outside Japan, sending representatives abroad to engage in diplomacy and study. In 1860, the bakufu dispatched seventy-seven men to the United States to exchange ratifications of the 1858 commercial treaty. Two years later it sent a similar embassy to Europe. Other, smaller missions followed. The impact of these journeys was monumental. Often the Japanese travelers were amazed by practices that seemed barbaric or just strange: museum displays of human bodies (mummies), people who did not bathe daily, men opening doors for women, and the worship of bloody Christian icons (crucifixes). At other times, the Japanese marveled at Western progress. On the 1862 mission, Fukuchi was stunned by newspapers that turned events into print overnight and embarrassed by the thousand pairs of straw sandals his superiors had packed in their ignorance of European train transportation. He gasped at a Paris hotel's dining hall, which could feed three thousand people. The economy may have produced the most fruitful Tokugawa initiatives. Reversing seclusionist policies, the bakufu encouraged pragmatic responses to the Western initiative. When foreigners used Japan's valuable silver coins to buy up vast sums of gold in 1859, the bakufu devalued the gold coins and ended the outflow. When the Europeans and Americans undersold Japanese cotton, officials allowed Japanese merchants to begin buying the imports instead of local cotton. The result was a sometimes disruptive but always dynamic shift in Japan's economy. Domestic silk prices rose, but sales declined, rising commodity prices led to rural uprisings, and local cotton producers suffered. Yet the economy expanded overall, with trade tripling between 1857 and 1865. Although full-scale capitalist expansion lay in the future, it was clear by the late 1860s that fundamental changes were under way.

In the end, the challenges were too great, and the Tokugawa were toppled by a coup d'état early in 1868. But their attempts to save themselves—and Japan—had a profound impact. Tokugawa officials did more than sign trade agreements. They opened Japan to the West. They created a new diplomacy. They stimulated public debates about Japan's role in the world. And they precipitated a dramatic revision of domestic political arrangements. If they could not rescue themselves, they nonetheless saved Japan from the imperialist depredations experienced by so many other countries. And they laid the foundations for even more radical transformations during the coming era.

2

THE MEIJI ORDER: ESTABLISHING BORDERS (1868-1890)

Crowds of Ryūkyū (present-day Okinawa) islanders stood in the dusk as Japanese soldiers escorted their thirty-five-year-old king, Sho Tai, away from his castle on March 30, 1879. Sho Tai's ancestors had ruled this Pacific kingdom for four centuries, maintaining its independence by balancing the demands of China to the west and Japan's Satsuma domain to the north. The independence struggle had grown difficult during the last decade, however, as Japan carved out its place in the imperial world. When the Japanese ordered the islanders to break off relations with China in 1875, Sho Tai quietly resisted. When they told him to come to Tokyo, to pay respects to the Japanese emperor, he claimed illness and stayed put. Now the troops were taking him by force. With ninety-six attendants, he sailed for Tokyo in May, announcing as a face-saving gesture that he was acting on the advice of Chinese officials. Japan turned his kingdom into Okinawa prefecture that spring. Ryūkyūan sovereignty became a memory. Although the king was allowed to visit his old home five years later, he remained a hostage until his death in 1901.

Sho Tai's plight dramatized how much Japan had changed in the decade after the Tokugawa fall. The country's new leaders had decided to emulate the imperialist powers rather than merely responding to them. A group of samurai and courtiers, mostly from the southwestern domains of Chōshū and Satsuma, claimed power in a bloodless coup d'état known as the Meiji Restoration on January 3, 1868, announcing that the Emperor Meiji was taking authority back from the Tokugawa family. The shogun fought back briefly, then surrendered, and despite eighteen months of bloody resistance by his followers the rebels had control of the central government by the spring of 1868. More quickly than anyone would have thought possible, they set Japan on the road to revolutionary reform.

The threats that confronted the Meiji leaders were monumental. The foreigners were still there, challenging Japan with what one Tokyo journalist called the imperialist creed: "Every man in the world strives for his own

11

advantage, regardless of the injuries inflicted upon others."[1] Staggering Tokugawa debts remained unpaid, regional lords wanted power, the military was ineffective, the industrial sector was nonexistent, and the new leaders had no experience in running a nation. Nonetheless, the Meiji rulers exuded confidence, partly because of their activist natures and partly because they knew the country also had strengths. The samurai heritage, for example, had left the country with a competent administrative class, well schooled in the idea of public service. The commercial sector was thriving, and the populace was highly literate by world standards. Moreover, the West offered a plethora of models that should speed the path to power.

Of crucial importance, the new regime was led by talented, pragmatic men, young rebels who may have been inexperienced but shared a unified vision. When the thirty-five-year-old leader Kido Kōin wrote after the Restoration that he expected Japan to become "the first-ranking nation of the world," he meant it.[2] Their hardheaded realism was exemplified in their approach toward the West. Although most of these men had belonged to expel-the-foreigner factions, now they adopted Westerners as mentors. Among their new slogans were *kuni no tame* (for the good of the country), *bunmei kaika* (civilization and enlightenment), and *fukoku kyōhei* (rich country/strong army). If something appeared useful, they pursued it, if not, they discarded it.

This approach produced a forty-five year era of breathtaking change, presaged in an 1868 Charter Oath that promised to eradicate "evil customs of the past," unify "all classes, high and low," create "deliberative assemblies," and seek "knowledge... throughout the world."[3] One of the first changes was the relocation of the emperor (who still had little power) from Kyoto to Edo, now renamed Tokyo. Another was the creation of patriotic symbols, including national holidays and a reinvigorated Shinto religion, which emphasized the emperor's sacred nature. The Meiji leaders also restructured the daimyo domains into prefectures. And they created a military draft, standardized the land tax system, and issued the world's first national law requiring all children to go to school. The result was a remarkable transformation of Japan's urban landscape, which by the late 1870s was brimming with brick buildings, barbershops, mailboxes, telegraph poles, women wearing evening gowns, men hawking newspapers, and restaurants offering meat and beer.

The most surprising evidence of the new leaders' pragmatism may have lain in the way they treated their own samurai class. For centuries warriors had lived off government stipends, provided in exchange for protecting and administering the domains. Now those stipends posed a huge financial burden even as they belied the Charter Oath's promise to unify classes. So in January 1876 the government disbanded the samurai class by prohibiting the wearing of swords and replacing stipends with one final, interest-bearing bond. Many samurai families fell into poverty, and others rose in armed opposition, with the vicious Satsuma Rebellion of 1877 claiming more than thirty thousand lives. But the move went far in rationalizing the administrative structure. Henceforth, ex-samurai would have to fight with words rather than swords.

Fig. 2.1. The influential editor Fukuchi Gen'ichirō, dressed in his typical dandified Western style, was sketched by the artist Kobayashi Kiyochika while reporting on the Satsuma Rebellion in 1877. (Courtesy of *Mainichi Shimbun*.)

The Meiji government's reform policies brought remarkable new energy to Japan's public spaces, with journalists arguing over every conceivable issue, writers experimenting with fresh literary forms, and women demanding a voice in national life. The centerpiece of the drive to modernity—and the effort that most energized the editorialists—was the move toward constitutionalism. Prodded by an emerging popular rights movement and a determination to earn international respect, the leaders concentrated after the late 1870s on creating a "modern" government. When an 1881 corruption scandal unleashed charges that the authorities were bent on personal gain, the government responded by promising a legislature within nine years. And in 1889 the emperor promulgated the Meiji Constitution, creating Asia's first constitutional monarchy. Drawn up with German advice, the document placed sovereignty in the emperor and provided for a strong executive, balanced by a relatively weak legislature, called the Diet, and an independent judiciary. The constitution encapsulated the Meiji essence, calling on mythical imperial traditions to guarantee the power of strong rulers while providing for a limited (but unstoppable) expansion of popular rights. Yamagata Aritomo, the architect of the Meiji military, toasted the promulgation with a boast: "In slightly over twenty years our political and cultural life has made . . . an advance unparalleled in the world."[4] What he did not toast, nor likely realize, was that the constitution's careful balancing of powers—deliberately making relationships between the legislature and the executive ambiguous—would provide an opening in later decades for the army and other groups to exert inordinate influence within the government.

Serving as a backdrop to these new policies was a swelling trend in international affairs, what scholars call the "new imperialism." All along the China coast, Western powers spent the late 1800s carving out spheres of influence. Elsewhere in Asia, they were taking over Indochina, India, the East Indies (Indonesia), Burma, and Malaya. And farther west they were turning ninety percent of Africa into colonies. Watching carefully, the Meiji leaders resolved that Japan would avoid the same fate. That was the reason for most of their modernizing policies. And it was the reason for a new approach to foreign affairs, which led both to determined efforts at clarifying national borders and to more aggressive diplomacy.

The diplomats focused on the effort to revise the unequal treaties, which deprived the government of desperately needed tariff revenues and reminded people constantly of foreign dominance. The issue was highlighted in 1879 when officials forbade a cholera-infected German ship from discharging passengers in Yokohama. The Germans ignored the order, pointing out that extraterritoriality deprived Japan of jurisdiction over foreigners, and nearly one hundred thousand Japanese died in an ensuing epidemic. The press's outrage was predictable.

The revision efforts took many forms, some direct and some indirect. In the latter category, Meiji leaders showed an astute understanding of the relationship between foreign respect and diplomatic success. In 1871, for example, they dispatched fifty leading officials on the eighteen-month Iwakura Mission to

America and Europe to report on the country's accomplishments and undertake treaty negotiations. When Germany's chancellor Otto von Bismarck warned them that strong nations used international law to their own ends, they listened. In the summer of 1872, when a Peruvian ship arrived in Japanese waters with more than two hundred Chinese workers crowded below deck in slavelike conditions, Tokyo officials saw a chance to show the world Japan's grasp of international law and set the workers free. The ship's owners protested, but international arbitrators backed Tokyo and the Western powers hailed Japan's handling of the affair. The government also subsidized sympathetic English-language newspapers in Tokyo and Yokohama in the 1870s, a telling sign of how well they understood the importance of a good public image.

Fig. 2.2. Matthew Brady took this photo of Itō Hirobumi (seated at left) during the 1872 visit of the Iwakura Mission to the United States. Itō, who later became prime minister and then served as Japan's first resident general of Korea, posed with unidentified colleagues. (Courtesy of the U.S. National Archives.)

At the direct level, early Meiji officials engaged in continuous negotiations to revise the unequal treaties. The work was slow because the powers were determined to maintain their advantages. In 1878, Japan and the United States reached a tentative agreement on tariff autonomy, but British opposition scuttled it. In the early 1880s, the government tried various approaches: multination conferences, negotiations with individual nations, and adoption of a mixed-court system with Japanese and foreign judges sitting together in cases involving foreigners. Each effort stalled, often because of British resistance, sometimes because of domestic opposition to concessions. But Japan's negotiators were indefatigable, refusing to let up until they were able finally to end extraterritoriality (in 1899) and abolish tariff limits (1911).

Japan generally avoided the imperialist path in the early Meiji years, but paid close attention to territorial issues, both to establishing clear borders and to defining its relations with neighbors. The first exercise in border fixing occurred in the north, where the island of Ezo was renamed Hokkaidō in 1869. Having been certified as Japanese territory in an 1855 treaty between Japan and Russia, the area now was placed under a Hokkaidō Colonization Office, with an annual development budget of a million yen. Across a decade, the office established an agricultural college, underwrote silk farms and beer factories, and supported modern farming. It also provided financial inducements for thousands of farmers and ex-samurai to move to Hokkaidō, including a contingent of two thousand from Totsukawa village in Nara prefecture following a disastrous flood. Unfortunately, the programs devastated Hokkaidō's native Ainu population. Many were pushed off their land by the immigrants; many more had their culture snatched away by Japan's assimilation policies. The Japanese "imposed difficulties," said one old man, recalling his grandparents' encounter with the incomers. "Trying to live on too little food, they died from malnutrition," he said. "Today only two or three Ainu families remain. . . . The others died out or fled." [5]

Even if the takeover was harsh, few questioned Japan's claim over Hokkaidō. The same could not be said about the Ryūkyūs. The Meiji regime decided quite early to challenge the seventy-island kingdom's independence. In 1872, Meiji authorities informed the international community that they considered it a Japanese domain. Two years later they used the Ryūkyūs as the pretext for a military mission to Taiwan. The trigger for the expedition was the massacre of fifty-four Ryūkyūan sailors by mountain peoples in southern Taiwan. When China disclaimed responsibility over the murderers, Japan sent three thousand troops, declaring that the misdeed must be punished. Military victory came easily in a dramatic battle fought in a mountain river between two rocky cliffs, followed by a short pacification campaign. The postwar negotiations were much more difficult, but when China signed a treaty describing the expedition as "just," the Meiji government took that as Chinese support for its claim of sovereignty over the Ryūkyūs. Some scholars argue that the Meiji leaders wanted to make Taiwan a colony, citing journalists such as Kishida Ginkō at *Tokyo Nichi Nichi Shimbun* who predicted that, in Taiwan, "the territory of the Japanese nation will be increasingly enlarged, frontiers opened, and trade enriched."[6] Others deny that Japan's leaders had colonial aims. There is no question, however, that the expedition was intended primarily to confirm Japan's control of the Ryūkyūs.

The absorption of the islands took five years. In 1875, Japan ordered the Ryūkyūans to stop sending tribute to China. Then four years later Sho Tai was abducted, and Tokyo began levying unusually high taxes on the Ryūkyūan people. Many islanders resisted bitterly, but to no avail, and by the middle of the Meiji period Japanese sovereignty was unassailable. Two other borders were completed in the 1870s: the Kuril Islands as far north as Kamchatka, secured through an 1875 treaty in exchange for Russian control of Sakhalin Island; and the Bonin Islands south of Tokyo, annexed in 1876.

The period's other major foreign focus was Korea, where Japan began working out its relations with the continent. Things got off to a difficult start in 1869 when Korean officials sent a Japanese envoy home for referring to Meiji as an emperor; he was a king, the Koreans said, as only the Chinese had emperors. More serious troubles threatened in 1873, when a "subdue Korea" faction in Tokyo secured approval of a mission to Korea considered likely to provoke war. When moderate officials succeeded in reversing the plan, the influential Saigō Takamori—who thought a military altercation would give new purpose to the old samurai class—left the government and returned to Kyushu, where he eventually led the Satsuma Rebellion. Three years later Japanese envoys, backed by gunboats, forced Korea to sign its first commercial treaty over the objections of one Korean official, who urged his king to "attack the evil and dirty [scum], so they will not dare to squat all over our borders."[7] As unequal as the imperialist agreements forced on Japan, the treaty opened three ports for trade, recognized Korea as a sovereign state (i.e., not dependent on China), and set the stage for two decades of Sino-Japanese struggle over influence in the peninsula.

The moves in Korea involved no territorial designs, but they demonstrated that Japan was determined to establish a secure place in the imperialist world. The maneuvers in Korea and the Ryūkyūs—which were designated as Okinawa Prefecture in 1879—showed a country ready to impose harsh conditions on weaker states. And the public discussions of each territorial move were couched in the hierarchical language so often used by Western imperialists. In the 1880s, the scholar Fukuzawa Yukichi described the Chinese and Koreans as "deep in their hocus pocus of nonscientific behavior" and recommended that Japan "leave the ranks of Asian nations and cast our lot with civilized nations of the West."[8] Others called for "civilizing" Korea. One group, including the women's rights pioneer Fukuda Hideko, went so far in 1885 as to gather weapons for an armed uprising intended to bring reform to Seoul. The plot was discovered and the conspirators were jailed, but their eagerness to force modernity on Korea revealed a people whose psychological boundaries had expanded. This might not be a time for militarist expansion. But clearly a new consciousness was developing. Other Asian lands might be backward and passive; Japan would be advanced and active. In the day's social Darwinist rhetoric, Japan must be fit if it were to survive. And fitness, it would turn out, meant embracing the imperialist logic in all its fullness.

3

THE IMPERIALIST TURN
(1890–1905)

osano Akiko already was a sensation when she published an antiwar poem in September 1904, having gained national attention by running away from her respectable shopkeeper's family to take up with a well-known poet. Her frank discussions of sensuality in a poetry collection named *Tangled Hair* also had gained her notoriety. Even her fans, however, were unprepared for this new work, which urged her brother not to die in battle. "Oh my little brother, I weep for you," she wrote, "And beg you: do not die. . . . His imperial majesty—he himself / Enters not the field of battle. / So vast and deep his sacred heart: / He cannot wish for you to spill / Your own blood and another's."[1]

Published while thousands of Japanese soldiers were falling in a war against Russia, the poem provoked accusations of treason. But Yosano would not back down. The mother of eleven and a traveler of the world, she showcased a Japan that made the early Meiji years seem inward looking by contrast. Her land was engaged now in an exhausting war with one of the European powers. It had become a colony holder. And it stood on the brink of developing its own full-fledged empire—Dai Nihon Teikoku in the parlance of the day, "Great Imperial Japan."

The attitudes responsible for that shift had proliferated in the late 1880s and early 1890s, when worries about survival gave way to debates about expansion. Nationalistic themes were heard everywhere now, with popular journals talking about Japan's mission and politicians hailing Meiji successes. The newspaper *Nihon* set the tone with criticisms of "Eurocentrism" and calls for "the revival and proclamation of the unique spirit of the Japanese people, handed down across the generations." After 1890, schoolchildren were required to recite an Imperial Rescript on Education (in the style of the American Pledge of Allegiance), promising to be "good and faithful subjects" and "guard and maintain the prosperity of Our Imperial Throne coeval with heaven and earth."[2]

This nationalist turn was accompanied by increasing calls for territorial aggrandizement. In 1887, for example, the political theorist Nakae Chōmin published a widely read treatise, *A Discourse by Three Drunkards*, in which he satirically has the most aggressive "drunkard" urge Japan to take over an African or Asian nation, for "by seizing it, we would change our nation from small to large, from weak to strong, and from poor to rich. . . . We'll pay a huge sum of money to buy the fruits of civilization." Others wrote about sending immigrants to Pacific islands or colonizing those regions. The journalist Shiga Shigetaka wrote in 1890 that Japan should mark the first emperor's accession and death anniversaries each year by taking territory. "Our naval vessels should on each of those days sail to a still unclaimed island, occupy it, and hoist the Rising Sun," he wrote, an act that "would excite an expeditionary spirit in the demoralized Japanese race."[3] Similar, if less bombastic, rhetoric was heard in official circles. In 1890, for example, Prime Minister Yamagata opened the new Diet with a speech asserting that to remain independent Japan must maintain both a "line of sovereignty" (the homeland) and a "line of advantage" (a buffer zone). Korea, he made clear, should be the buffer zone. He did not recommend conquest, but he did insist that it be protected from Chinese or Russian domination.

In 1894, several conditions provided an opportunity to act on Yamagata's idea. Domestically, Japan was in political turmoil, with opposition parties attacking the government over a host of issues, including its difficulties in achieving treaty revision. Abroad, Russia's growing involvement in eastern Asia was stirring up increasing concern. Then, in May, Korea provoked an avalanche of debate by asking China to help suppress a peasant-based religious group, the Tonghaks, which had fomented a peninsula-wide rebellion against government corruption and the spread of foreign influences (particularly Christianity).

When China sent fifteen hundred soldiers to the peninsula, Japanese editorialists accused Beijing of violating Korean independence, even though the Chinese had acted in accordance with Sino-Japanese treaties. Writer after writer demanded that Japan send troops, and after prolonged discussions the cabinet agreed. By late June, Tokyo had dispatched eight thousand men. By July, hostilities were under way. And on August 1, Japan declared war on China, backed by a public anxious about taking on Asia's largest nation yet charged with patriotism. Fukuzawa's newspaper, *Jiji Shinpō*, wrote, "Whatever happens, whatever the difficulties, our nation's forty millions are resolved not to withdraw one step until exhausted, and, whatever the cost, to prevail."[4] People need not have worried about the military challenge because China presented none. The war's only shadow came when Japanese troops massacred civilians after taking Manchuria's Port Arthur in November. By early 1895, Japan had triumphed on every front. The peace treaty, signed on April 17, established Japan as East Asia's leading power.

As so often in war, the most important results sprang from the currents that surrounded (and followed) it. For one thing, the war inspired a wave of patriotism. Early Meiji officials had worked hard, with uneven results, to inculcate a national spirit in the populace; now patriotism spread like an epidemic. The war also made Japan richer, both materially and geographically, thanks to a generous peace settlement. Having lost every battle, China had no negotiating leverage, and the resultant Treaty of Shimonoseki gave Japan all that it demanded: a recognition of Korea's independence, special commercial rights in China, an indemnity of nearly 350 million yen, and a great deal of territory, including the Pescadore Islands, Taiwan, and the southern Manchurian peninsula known as Liaodong. The indemnity underwrote all of Japan's war expenses; the territory turned the country into an empire. The "new imperialism" was no longer a Western monopoly.

Fig. 3.1. Japan's national mood as the end of the Sino-Japanese War approached was clear in this *Jiji Shinpō* editorial cartoon (January 1, 1895) showing a diminutive but agile Japanese soldier exulting over a huge Chinese rival. The text proclaimed, "Cheers to Great Imperial Japan, Cheers to Their Majesties, Cheers to the Army and Navy." (Courtesy of Meiji Shimbun Zasshi Bunkō.)

The Sino-Japanese War also inspired new talk of military expansion, in part because of the way several Western powers responded to Japan's victory. On April 23, just six days after the treaty signing, Russia, Germany, and France urged Japan to return the Liaodong Peninsula to China, warning that its retention would threaten East Asia's peaceful balance. As the Japanese knew, the real reason for this "triple intervention" was cynical; Russia, in particular, had its own designs on that region. Nonetheless, the cabinet was not ready to challenge Russia, so Liaodong was returned in exchange for a 15 percent increase in the indemnity. And the public erupted in rage, declaring that weakness must never again dictate diplomacy. The phrase of choice over the next few years was "*gashin shōtan*" (perseverance and determination). Japan must be strong enough to *act* like an imperial power, even against European giants.

The years following the Sino-Japanese War revealed a country transformed as early Meiji institutions matured. The economy grew remarkably, if not evenly, with millions of yen poured into railroads, factories, and communications networks. Trade increased nearly tenfold between 1887 and 1920, and personal consumption doubled. Cities seethed with new life as department stores, movie theaters, and beer halls appeared, while electric trolleys and trains competed with forty thousand rickshaw pullers to move people around. Both Osaka and Tokyo drew tourists with multi-story observation towers that offered Japan's first elevators. The cities also produced sprawling slums, where job seekers from the countryside crowded together in one-room apartments without indoor kitchens or toilets, while ragpickers and bar waitresses slept in flophouses, struggling to survive on wages that "sprout wings and fly away like a butterfly, or a bee, or a locust."[5] Modernity had arrived with all of its complexity.

The changes affected international affairs, too. If trade pulled Japan into the world economic system, the determination to be a continental actor transformed diplomacy. Near at hand, Japan poured resources into Korea, attempting in a clear case of imperialism without colonization to modernize the infrastructure and establish a continental foothold. But other powers were interested in Korea, too, and the process proved frustrating. When Miura Gorō arrived in Seoul as Japan's minister in September 1895, he decided to install a pro-Japanese government, by force if necessary. Without authorization from Tokyo, he had the anti-Japanese Queen Min assassinated on the evening of October 7. The move backfired, however. Foreign governments protested, Tokyo recalled Miura, and Korea's King Kojong turned north for assistance, taking up residence the following February in the Russian embassy.

A similar combination of activism and frustration typified Japan's global role more generally. At home, the government quadrupled military spending, putting feet to *gashin shōtan*. In China, there was little the Japanese could do but look on in frustration, as Russia used treaties to take control of Liaodong, the very region it had forced Japan to return to China. Then in 1900, Japan saw its international reputation rise again when it contributed ten thousand troops to the international force that ended China's Boxer Rebellion, winning another indemnity and the right to station soldiers in Beijing. And in 1902 it countered Russia's advances in eastern Asia by signing an alliance with the British that recognized Japanese predominance in Korea and British preeminence in China. Few doubted, by the early 1900s, that Japan had become a world power; fewer still remained naive about the complications of life among the imperialist elite.

This complexity was particularly clear in Taiwan—the colony gained in the Sino-Japanese War settlement. Japan had ambitious plans for the island as a defense base and a source of raw materials (and markets) for Japan's expanding economy. It was also a test case, where Japan could demonstrate its skill in running a colony. After a brutal campaign to subdue Taiwanese resisters, which claimed many thousands of lives on each side, the first three governors struggled to overcome endless policy disagreements in Tokyo and

Fig. 3.2. A Taiwanese farmer cultivates his fields behind a water buffalo, playing his part in bringing energy to the island's economy under Japan's colonial agricultural policies. (Courtesy of the U.S. National Archives.)

their own lack of colonial administrative experience, running up financial debts that left many asking whether colony holding was too heavy a burden. By decade's end, however, things had turned around under the brilliant young administrator Gotō Shinpei. Adopting "scientific" policies based on research into local conditions, Gotō combined harsh control and heavy taxes with aggressive development of Taiwan's infrastructure in health, communications, banking, education, and transportation. He also attracted effective assistants, including the Quaker Nitobe Inazō, whose agricultural policies produced dramatic increases in sugar production. Gotō was less successful in attracting private Japanese investment, but by 1904 Taiwan had become self-sufficient and was being praised as a model of imperial administration. A Diet member predicted that the successes would make Japan "Queen of the Pacific."[6]

Ironically, each expansive step increased Japan's sense of vulnerability. If acquisitions brought prestige and power, they also attracted enemies, raising fresh controversies and increasing Japan's sense of isolation. Nowhere was this more evident than in relations with Russia. After Russia secured control over southern Manchuria in 1898, commentators began discussing the "shame of Liaodong," and when Russian troops moved into Manchuria after the Boxer Rebellion, the writers discerned a Russian threat. Then, when Russia failed in 1903 to follow a promised timetable for withdrawing troops from Manchuria, many demanded a response, amplifying a widely discussed call by seven University of Tokyo professors to use force if necessary to remove Russia from Manchuria. The tone recalled the press's tirades against China a decade earlier.

The result was Japan's second imperialist war, begun on February 8, 1904, with an attack on Russia's Port Arthur fleet and fought between two major powers over Korea, a land not their own, for reasons that had more to do with security and prestige than economics. This conflict was more difficult than the war with China: massively expensive, requiring huge loans from the Americans and Europeans; much longer, consuming nineteen months; more brutal, taking the lives of a quarter of a million troops; and less decisive. Japan won the major battles, first at Port Arthur, then at Shenyang (Mukden), but by the time it inflicted a decisive defeat on Russia's fleet in the Tsushima Straits between Japan and Korea in late May 1905, its resources were largely spent. One would hardly have known that from Japanese press reports, most of which wrapped the struggles in heroic prose. But the war's realities were ambiguous. Even among journalists, the war evoked a smattering of doubt, with socialists advocating peace and thinkers such as Yosano asking whether the carnage was worth it. When a treaty—signed at Portsmouth, New Hampshire—ended the war on September 4, 1905, tens of thousands across the country opposed its terms in demonstrations that often turned violent. Very few, including the rioters, questioned Japan's move toward imperialism, but many had begun having doubts about some of the ramifications of the great power game.

The main trigger for the questioning was the peace treaty. Historians generally give Japan's negotiators at Portsmouth solid marks, partly because of their realistic flexibility on contentious issues and partly because of their success in securing for Japan the Russian rights in southern Manchuria, sovereignty ("in perpetuity") over the southern half of Sakhalin, and recognition of Japan's "preponderant interest" in Korea. But the negotiators were excoriated at home. Conditioned by wartime rhetoric, the public was outraged that the peace provided for neither an indemnity nor much territory in Russia's far east. After "spending as much as two billion yen" and "suffering deaths and casualties . . . this is all we get!" wrote a subscriber to the newspaper *Asahi*. "This is nonsense! We people should demand that our government pay us for our losses."[7]

While the anger eventually subsided, the commitment to expansion did not; nor did the complexities introduced by the growing imperialist habit. To the far north, the treaty added a new colony, southern Sakhalin, which the Japanese called Karafuto, and to the near west it started Japan down the path that would make Korea a third colony. That path would be tortuous, but Japan would stay the course this time, determined to create an unassailable buffer zone. The Russo-Japanese War thus proved pivotal in Japan's imperial evolution. It increased the country's colonial holdings. It deepened the conviction that modernity entailed empire building. And it sent Japan farther into the international power game, involving it in the miasma of continental politics, raising Western suspicions, and, in the analysis of Keiō University historian Yokote Shinji, helping to "end the European-dominated politics of this region and promote the collapse of the old order."[8] The full implications of the new direction would become clear only later. What was clear in the autumn of 1905 was that the basic goals of Meiji imperialism now had been secured; Japan had protected itself against foreign threats and gained respect as a world power.

4

PURSUING THE LOGIC OF EMPIRE
(1905–1919)

Prison officials found twenty-three-year-old Kaneko Fumiko hanging from a hemp rope of her own making. Convicted of plotting to kill the emperor, she demonstrated by her defiant 1926 death that nationalists no longer monopolized Japan's intellectual world. And her life course shed light on the direction in which imperialism had begun taking Japan, for it was a seven-year sojourn in Korea during the 1910s that turned her into an anarchist. Born into poverty in Yokohama, Kaneko was sent as a child to live with relatives who were working as colonial officials in Korea. There she grew to hate a grandmother who, on a typical day, beat her and locked her in a grain shed simply for visiting the home of a lower-class schoolmate. Of the day when the family humiliated a servant for requesting time off to care for his family, she recalled, "I hated my grandmother and aunt out of a sense of pure justice more at that moment than I ever have in my whole life."[1] When Kaneko returned to Japan in 1919, she was a revolutionary anticolonialist. Her fellow countrymen, by contrast, were enthusiasts of empire—whenever they thought of anything besides their own daily lives.

The teenage Kaneko's Japan was a lively place. Under the Emperor Taishō, who took the throne in 1912, the country witnessed the rise of an urban middle class that pursued nationalism and personal prosperity with equal avidity. These were years of labor activism, of tenant unions, of consumerism and department stores, years that found people thronging public spaces, sometimes chatting at street-side cafés, other times protesting high streetcar fares. "Never since the dawn of world history has the growth of the individual been so respected and material happiness so sought after," wrote the social critic Ukita Kazutami.[2] Not surprisingly, officials found many of these developments unnerving, but none of their programs to encourage consensus or traditional values could check the day's most conspicuous feature: debate and innovation.

One of the key debate topics was what approach Japan should take to empire. The day's leading opinion journal, *Taiyō*, which had concentrated on domestic issues prior to the Russo-Japanese War, brimmed now with articles on Japan's role in Asia. A few worried that Japan's foreign acquisitions had unleashed uncontrollable forces, but most favored continued expansion, even as the military sought higher budgets. Ukita, far from the most chauvinist commentator, called for Japan to bring "civilization and prosperity" to more distant regions such as Latin America. "Why," he asked in 1910, "are not the Japanese race prepared to make a leap in this New World, rather than to be left confined in their small world of the Far West?"[3] The logic of empire for him was clear, as it was for most officials: strengthen control of what Japan already had; advance when opportunity presented itself.

The practical working out of this approach occurred first in Korea, where Japan began taking control even while war with Russia was still raging. Itō Hirobumi, one of the dominant Meiji political figures, was sent to Seoul in the fall of 1905 to make Korea into a protectorate. Backed by his country's military, he coerced Seoul into signing a treaty in November making Japan responsible for Korean governance and diplomacy. He insisted that Korea would remain "independent" and predicted that it eventually would achieve equality with Japan, but by the summer of 1907 Japan had disbanded Korea's army and forced King Kojong to abdicate, all with the support of the other imperialist powers. When Kojong sent representatives to a 1907 Hague peace conference to protest Japan's takeover, the delegates refused to listen. Wrote the *New York Tribune*, "The Law of survival of the fittest prevails among states as well as among plants and animals. Corea has been conspicuously unfit."[4]

Itō also set out to modernize Korea, carrying out a costly program of revamping the tax and postal systems, building railways and telegraph lines, and encouraging industry. Unfortunately for the Koreans, it was the Japanese who benefited most from the reforms, at least in the short term. By 1910, nearly 150,000 Japanese had moved to the peninsula, almost half of them in business, the rest ranging the spectrum of professions: bureaucrats, reporters, attorneys, farmers, teachers. By then, Korean fishing waters had been opened to the Japanese, too, as had mining and timber rights, and the government-sponsored Oriental Development Company was providing capital for agricultural and industrial projects. While the company had a hard time persuading industrialists to invest, small businessmen came in significant numbers. And Japanese farmers bought up as much as 10 percent of the arable land in some regions, helping to stimulate a growing trade that was much to Japan's benefit.

Fig. 4.1. After two decades of Japanese control, Korean farmers daily brought great quantities of rice to the port at Inchon, bagged and ready to be shipped to Japan and other countries. (Courtesy of the U.S. National Archives.)

Fig. 4.2. Japan's modernizing policies in the 1910s and 1920s turned Seoul into an increasingly modern city with electric lines, railway tracks, and Model Ts, alongside horse-drawn carts and pedestrians. (Courtesy of the U.S. National Archives.)

If Itō expected a repeat of Japan's success in quelling the resistance in Taiwan a decade earlier, he was disappointed. While many Koreans cooperated with the Japanese, others fought. When the protectorate was negotiated, significant numbers of Korean officials refused to cooperate; some committed suicide. And as Japan tightened its control, great numbers joined the opposition. Across the land, local bands staged armed uprisings, frequently under the command of former soldiers. In one episode, nearly ten thousand "righteous army" troops marched to within eight miles of Seoul before Japanese forces defeated them. By Japan's own official estimates, twenty-five thousand Koreans and Japanese had died in the fighting by 1910.

The most dramatic act of resistance led to the end of Korea's claims even to nominal independence. When the patriot An Chung-gun shot Itō to death while he was traveling in Manchuria in October 1909, Japan decided to annex the peninsula. Korea thus became the country's third colony on August 29, 1910. For Koreans, this was history's bleakest moment. For Japan, annexation gave deeper meaning to the word "empire." For the Western powers, it was imperialism as usual. As Theodore Roosevelt advised President William Howard Taft a few months later, America should do nothing to "give the Japanese cause to feel . . . that we are hostile to them" because "our vital interest is to keep the Japanese out of our country and at the same time to preserve the good will of Japan."[5]

One reason for Roosevelt's attitude lay in the fact that Japan was acting much like the other imperial powers; another was that Japan's international role had become more complex. It now boasted East Asia's strongest navy, it was demonstrating a growing interest in China, and it was projecting a larger trade profile, as well as sending immigrants around the globe. Just four years earlier Roosevelt had worked out the sensitive Gentleman's Agreement, in which Japan agreed to prohibit laborers from migrating to the continental United States if San Francisco would not place Japanese workers' children in segregated schools. Pressured by anti-immigrant sentiment on the West Coast, Roosevelt and Taft would go along with Japanese moves in Asia if Japan would help them placate critics at home. This was the imperialist world.

The expansiveness of Japan's foreign vision was apparent throughout eastern Asia and the Pacific during the 1910s. In Taiwan, the colonial regime's authoritarian approach was challenged at mid-decade by an "assimilation" (dōka) movement initiated by progressives who thought Taiwanese should be given greater political rights; after a two-year surge, however, the movement was crushed by colonial officials. Meanwhile, to the southeast, in the southern Pacific, Japan took its fourth colony, the German-held Micronesian chain of two thousand islands known as Nan'yō (South Seas). With Britain's hesitant approval, Japan invoked the Anglo-Japanese Alliance in the fall of 1914 and entered World War I, sending two naval squadrons to take over the largely defenseless islands. The move sparked disapproving comment in the United States, where anti-Japanese sentiments had been aroused by a combination of America's own designs on the Pacific and racist talk about a "yellow peril." But most Japanese lauded the takeover as an "appropriate" addition with potential strategic value. When the war ended, the Paris Peace Conference mandated the region to Japan, with an agreement that the islands would be administered as part of the homeland but would not be armed. Across the next decade, almost 950 Japanese officials took full control of the islands' administration. Japan's rule, says Nan'yō historian Mark Peattie, was "intensive and dominating."[6] It was relatively peaceful too, inciting little resistance.

Japan also became more active in China in the 1910s. After defeating German forces in Shandong province, Japan issued a set of twenty-one demands to China early in 1915, attempting to use the wartime milieu to more securely assure its place alongside the European powers. Most of

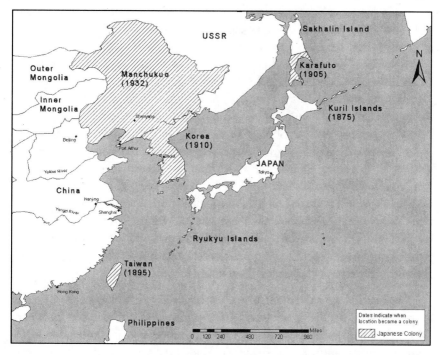

Map 2. The Evolution of Japan's Empire, 1875–1932. Japan also acquired Nan'yō—a collection of two-thousand islands in the south Pacific—in 1914. (Courtesy of Taylor Hafley.)

the demands were intended to strengthen positions Japan already held—to assure its control over the former German holdings in Shandong, extend its rights in Manchuria, and improve mining opportunities—but a controversial final set went further, proposing to put Japanese advisers into key Chinese government offices and to require China to buy arms from Japan. The demands outraged the Chinese, and after hard negotiations Japan dropped the final set and China's weak government accepted the rest. Although the agreement largely affirmed the status quo in China, it brought criticism from the Western powers, with U.S. president Woodrow Wilson, in particular, raising questions about Japanese opportunism. Less controversial in the West were Japan's activities in Manchuria, where the South Manchurian Railway Company and the Manchuria-based Guandong (Kwantung) Army, named for the region in which it operated, oversaw rapid development after the Russo-Japanese War. During the 1910s, Japan invested heavily in railways, mining, industry, and agriculture; it also involved itself in local governments along the railway corridor.

The hardheaded realism of Japan's maturing imperial goals may have been clearest in its relations with Russia. One might have expected pure enmity after the Russo-Japanese War; instead a conciliatory relationship ensued. Between 1907 and 1916, Japan and Russia signed a series of agreements promising to respect each other in their East Asian arenas, and during World War I Japan provided weapons to Russia in return for transportation concessions. Rapprochement, however, signified calculated self-interest, not friendship. The agreements involved a series of promises—signed in secret to avoid raising international opposition—to recognize each country's territorial claims in eastern Asia, including Russian support for Japan's activities in Korea and southern Manchuria, balanced by Japanese recognition of Russia's spheres in northern Manchuria and Outer Mongolia. Equally calculating was Japan's 1918 decision to send more than seventy thousand troops to Siberia, explicitly to assist in an Allied intervention against the country's new Communist government but more likely to create a buffer zone against the Soviets. The expedition failed disastrously, but its goals squared with Japan's consistent commitment in these years to strengthening its continental presence whenever international conditions made it feasible.

The heart of Japan's empire in the 1910s was Korea, which was dominated by competent, authoritarian bureaucrats who oversaw what the historian Bruce Cumings calls a blend of "development and underdevelopment, agrarian growth and deepened tenancy, industrialization and extraordinary dislocation, political mobilization and deactivation," all of which created "deep fissures and conflicts that have gnawed at the Korean soul ever since."[7]

The archetypal colonial administrator was Terauchi Masatake, the governor-general from 1910 to 1916, who continued Itō's modernization program but governed in an even harsher style. He directed a top-down administration in which thousands of Japanese civil servants wrote law codes, developed modern tax and land ownership systems, and oversaw daily life. They were assisted by a powerful police network (half Korean, half Japanese), which in turn was supported by the Japanese army. The police assisted in administration, too, making sure that rice was harvested, taxes were paid, and children went to school.

Although the Japanese poured more money into Korea than they had into Taiwan, economic development proceeded slowly in the 1910s. Rice production increased moderately, with much of the grain exported to Japan. And Korea's old landed elites, the *yangban*, gained a firmer hold on farm properties as a result of the land surveys, even as many illiterate farmers lost control of the land they had long tilled. The decade also saw increasing ownership, of both industries and land, by the Japanese, partly because private giants such as Mitsubishi began investing in factories and railroads and partly because the financial structures favored the incomers. The Bank of Korea, formed as a central bank in 1909, gave loans primarily to Japanese, and under the 1910 Company Law, nearly 90 percent of new business licenses went to Japanese. While some Korean entrepreneurs benefited from the economic policies, even more stagnated or fell on hard times.

The most notorious feature of Korean colonialism in the 1910s was Terauchi's heavy-handed approach to order: sword-bearing schoolteachers, policemen who whipped suspects arbitrarily, and arrogant officials who supported landlords over tenants. Popular resentment erupted in a mass protest early in 1919, which became known as the March First Incident. Following the issuance of a declaration of Korean independence by resistance leaders on March 1, as many as a million people from all walks of life demonstrated across the country, demanding freedom from Japanese rule. The Japanese, shocked by the scale of the protests, responded brutally, shooting into crowds, shutting down schools, even burning villages. Before the episode had subsided several months later, more than three thousand demonstrations had resulted in twenty thousand arrests and some two thousand deaths. The Korea historian Michael E. Robinson calls the episode "a shining moment of national unity during the long dark night of Japanese rule."[8]

One result of the protests was the growth of independence movements abroad, including a Korean government in exile in Shanghai. Another was a rush of soul-searching in Japan, where many questioned Terauchi's harsh approach. Only a few, however, expressed qualms about colonialism and imperialism themselves. Most agreed with the popular Tokyo University political theorist Yoshino Sakuzō, who decried the treatment of Koreans but insisted that Japan maintain control. In a decade that had witnessed secret arrangements with Russia, railroad building in Manchuria, expansion into Nan'yō, and demands for privileges in China, only a few entertained Kaneko's questions about the wisdom of the system. Modernity still entailed imperialism, and the logic of imperialism demanded the exercise of a firm hand in existing colonies and expansion at opportune moments.

5

QUIETER EXPANSION (1919–1929)

Although "Naomi" cared little about empires and colonies in the 1920s, she loved the things that imperialist countries produced. The dominant character in Tanizaki Jun'ichirō's 1924 novel by that name, she captured Japan—and represented an age—with her love of pleasure. "There was a picture of her dressed in a man's velvet suit," murmured her boyfriend, browsing an album. "On the next page, she stood like a statue, wrapped in cotton voile. On the next, she appeared in a glittering satin kimono and jacket. . . . Sometimes she looked like the actress Mary Pickford, sometimes like Pola Negri, and always like a party-goer."[1] Like so many in her decade, Naomi was obsessed with the personal and the pleasurable, driven by products and passions available only in a society that, while experiencing its first decade in four without war, continued to be heavily involved in global trade and politics.

Pluralism and energy permeated Japanese life now even more than it had in the 1910s. In seedy rooms and elegant lecture halls, intellectuals discussed Marxism, anarchism, capitalism, and democracy. In burgeoning industrial plants, workers (more than half of them women) staged increasing numbers of protest actions, while on the streets ragpickers and urchins made their class-conscious peers uncomfortable. Farther along the social spectrum, department stores offered Naomi's counterparts those fashionable dresses and beers, even as radios broadcast popular music and gossipy magazines sold a million copies an issue. And Asia's first subway system combined with automobiles and tram cars to move people about more quickly than ever before. By 1925, democracy had expanded, too, with the passage of universal male suffrage. "We can feel the air of a new era," wrote the novelist Kataoka Teppei.[2]

But while the young and the idealistic reveled in the dynamism, conservatives and officials worried about challenges to the traditional order. They responded with writings, laws, and programs intended to undercut the

Fig. 5.1. Hirohito, known in Japan as the Shōwa Emperor, ascended the throne in 1926, two years before this formal photo was taken. (*New York Times* Photos, courtesy of the U.S. National Archives.)

Left and promote loyalty to the state. Shinto campaigns heralded reverence for imperial ancestors, a literary award system encouraged wholesome writing, military training was added to the middle school curriculum, and the Home Ministry supported nationalist organizations such as the Greater Japan National Essence Association, formed to promote imperialism and fight labor activism. The government also passed a peace preservation law in 1925, forbidding the espousal of socialism and laying the groundwork for thought police, who would engage in draconian crackdowns on the Left in later years. The expression of diverse thought and the pursuit of pleasure continued into the 1930s. But each year saw increased efforts by the Right to strengthen national loyalty and curb what conservatives saw as liberal excesses. It was a heady but worrisome mixture.

Similar contradictions dominated Japan's external affairs in the 1920s, with a generally conciliatory foreign policy balanced by strong colonial control and an expansive, if relatively peaceful, approach to China. Nitobe, the one-time agricultural pioneer in Taiwan, gave an international face to the decade as undersecretary general of the League of Nations, where he argued that Japan should align itself with world opinion. Accordingly, Japan signed the 1928 Kellogg-Briand Pact, renouncing war as an instrument of national policy. And more crucially, Tokyo agreed to a naval pact in Washington in 1922, which restricted Japan to 60 percent of the warship tonnage allowed the Americans and British (a 5-5-3 formula), even though military experts insisted that Japan needed a minimum of 70 percent. In these years, Japan also normalized relations with the Soviet Union, removed troops from Siberia, and returned territories in Shandong to China.

None of this meant that the country's foreign ambitions had withered, however. Nor did it mean that support for conciliation was universal. Powerful officials such as Tanaka Giichi (prime minister, 1927–29) argued for greater assertiveness in Asia, as did leading military figures. And several Western moves stimulated criticism from both the Left and the Right. Woodrow Wilson's refusal to accept a racial equality clause in the Versailles peace treaty that ended World War I, for example, reinforced those who said Westerners were idealistic only when it suited their purposes. And when the United States forbade all Japanese immigration to America in 1924, even Nitobe declared that he would no longer visit it. Invited to speak at Columbia University seven years later, he responded, "Nothing will entice me to enter the country where my own kith and kin are not treated on equal terms with the rest of mankind."[3] His less pacifist compatriots argued that Japan must look out for itself in Asia if the powers denied them access to the West.

The tug-of-war between conciliation and strength was felt keenly in Korea. On the softer side, the uproar over the March First demonstrations in 1919 prompted concerted efforts to win Korean hearts through a policy called *bunka seiji* (cultural rule), which aimed at adapting policies to Korean ways of life. Military police were replaced with a civilian force, whipping was forbidden, officials stopped wearing military uniforms, more Koreans were employed in the colonial bureaucracy, and a Korean-language press was permitted. The result was a livelier Korean intellectual life, particularly in the early 1920s, and considerable economic growth. The press flourished, as hundreds of magazines and newspapers came into being. Nearly five thousand local organizations representing labor, religion, youth, and women were formed, and in 1927 the New Korea Society was launched to promote Korean unity and pride. In the economic sphere, rice production rose 40 percent in the 1920s, thanks in part to extensive new irrigation projects, and government subsidies helped to launch several Korean companies that over time would become hugely successful.

Japanese officials never wavered, however, in their determination to keep a firm hold on Korea. As in Taiwan, which saw a similar softening of administrative approaches, the authorities' goal was to maintain stability and feed Japan's own economy. Thus, while some Koreans benefited, others felt minimal (if any) improvement. Most business subsidies went to Japanese firms, the rest to strategic Korean companies inclined to cooperate with Japan. And, despite the rise in rice production, domestic consumption actually declined as farmers sent their harvests abroad and ate cheaper food themselves. In the field of security, while civilians replaced soldiers in local police forces, the overall size of those forces grew to more than eighteen thousand officers by 1926. Moreover, after 1925 colonial authorities used Japan's new Peace Preservation Law to clamp down on radicals. If colonial policy took on a gentler face in the 1920s, the reason was strategic, not a reflection of fundamental changes in goals.

The decade's greatest expansion occurred in a place that was not a formal colony: Manchuria. Even as it prodded tens of thousands of Japanese to move to Nan'yō and sent two hundred thousand immigrants to harvest the resources of Karafuto, Japan devoted its chief energies to creating an agricultural-industrial infrastructure in Northeast China. After securing the Russian leases there, Tokyo had used a combination of threats, diplomacy, and administrative skill to turn the region into an economic giant. One tool in the project was the military, which assigned roughly ten thousand Guandong Army troops to guard the railway lines and protect the Japanese community. The other was the South Manchurian Railway Company—typically referred to as Mantetsu—a semipublic firm founded with two hundred million yen in 1906 to oversee the railroad and develop the economy.[4]

Mantetsu soon became Japan's largest corporation. Headquartered in Dalian and presided over in its early years by Gotō Shinpei, who had experienced such success in Taiwan, it supervised a vast array of coal mines, ironworks, hotels, railroads, libraries, parks, sugar refineries, harbors, and a research wing that analyzed the colonial enterprise. It also handled the administration of a hundred towns and, by decade's end, boasted over a billion yen in assets. Considerable revenue came from the transportation of goods on trains that averaged a rapid thirty-five miles an hour, and the most profitable enterprise was soybeans. "The humble bean has been, and still is, the factor which determines the fortunes of the nations interested in Manchurian trade," wrote the journalist K. K. Kawakami.[5] By 1930, Mantetsu also had overseen the immigration of nearly a quarter of a million Japanese to Manchuria, which now was producing half of the world's soybeans.

Manchuria was not a colony, however, either in the technical sense or in Japan's rhetoric. The factors that prevented formal colonization lay mainly in the region's political milieu. In the early 1920s, China was a cauldron, led by an ineffective government under attack from various warlords and rebel groups. Although a civil war, which erupted in mid-decade, ended in 1928 with a shaky victory by the Nationalist forces of Chiang Kaishek (Jiang Jieshi), the government continued to face challenges from Communist forces across the country. Most problematic for the Japanese was the northeastern warlord Zhang Zuolin, who alternatively cooperated and competed with them. Mantetsu officials worked out repeated agreements, promising to support him as warlord in return for railway and commercial concessions.

Fig. 5.2. The Hungarian writer Edgar Lajtha took this photo of a team of Japanese scientists and agricultural experts examining one of the forty-four experimental farms that Japan developed in Manchuria in the 1920s and 1930s. Soybeans (right) proved especially profitable. (World Wide Photos, courtesy of the U.S. National Archives.)

They placed advisers in his government, provided him with financial and military assistance, and spoke of coexistence. But ultimately Zhang was not controllable. His schools competed with those the Japanese were constructing, he developed his own railroad and commercial ventures, and he worked to develop a power base throughout China. He also was less than vigilant in controlling the region's many anti-Japanese activists.

While the Mantetsu establishment continued to cooperate with Zhang, radical elements talked increasingly in the late 1920s about reining him in and turning the region into a colony. One of them, Colonel Kōmoto Daisaku, decided to speed things up in June 1928 by having Zhang's train bombed in the hope that Tokyo would replace the warlord with a puppet ruler and take full control of Manchuria. Things did not go as planned, however. Zhang died, but Tokyo refused to change course, and the warlord's successor son, Zhang Xueliang, launched even more vigorous challenges to the Japanese, cooperating with Chiang Kaishek's effort to bring Manchuria under full Chinese control. Anti-Japanese activism merely increased.

The decade thus came to a close in Northeast China with advocates of the status quo struggling against those who wanted Japan to be more aggressive. "We will not reach our objective if we simply follow the flow of events. . . . We must think of shaping the situation ourselves," maintained the expansionist prime minister to be, Tanaka Giichi. "There is no other course . . . than to pursue the path of mutual accord and cooperation," argued the conciliatory foreign minister, Shidehara Kijūrō.[6] No one, however, advocated the abandonment of Manchuria or of Nan'yō, Taiwan, Karafuto, or Korea. The post–World War I political climate may have prompted officials to don velvet gloves, but their fists remained firm. Japan was in the colonial business to stay.

6

THREE CRISES
(1929–1932)

Ishiwara Kanji's class in the history of European war was so popular at the Army Staff College that school officials asked him to expand it. Only twenty-six in 1926, the major had recently spent three years in Germany, studying military history and sharing conversations with a prominent follower of the militant thirteenth-century Buddhist prophet Nichiren, who envisioned Japan as the lever to save the world from end-times destruction. Now, Ishiwara argued, the end-times were approaching. The world was moving toward a final war—between Japan and the United States—in which "Japan must be victorious, not for the sake of her own national interest, but for the salvation of the world." If his country succeeded, "[O]ur powerful enemies will be vanquished, the glorious spirit of the Japanese *kokutai* [national polity] will come home to the hearts of the peoples of all nations, and the world will enter an era of peace under the guidance of the imperial throne."[1]

Although Ishiwara's ideas stirred many students and attracted key figures in the military—who had been convinced by Germany's loss in World War I that Japan must be stronger and more self-sufficient economically if it were to stand up to the great powers militarily—they were extreme and unlikely to flourish more broadly in the pluralistic 1920s. History, however, is a contingent thing, shaped often by the convergence of unpredictable events and the interplay of unforeseen (or unnoticed) forces. The brief span from 1929 to 1931 produced three such events, none of them predicted by most Taishō analysts, which made the national soil fertile for Ishiwara's theories and turned him into one of the decade's key actors, the leader of a growing group of what sometimes were called "total war officers."[2]

Event One. In October 1929, following the collapse of the New York Stock Exchange, the world plunged into the Great Depression. Economic nationalism swept both hemispheres, prompting protectionist trade policies, and world trade had plummeted by two-thirds by 1932. Millions on millions became jobless, wages fell for those still working, and people lost homes and went hungry. Nor was Japan immune. Over the next three years, farmers shuddered as agricultural prices dropped by 43 percent, silk prices declined by a third, and urban unemployment rates soared past 20 percent, prompting worker protests in unprecedented numbers. The farmers of northern Honshu were especially hard hit, as crop failures in 1931 and 1934 intensified the depression's impact. Half the people in one prefecture were reported to be on the edge of starvation; in another, a journalist described desperate farmers selling children. They "insist that they will never let their daughters go, even if they cannot eat," he wrote, "but the daughters say they cannot bear to see their parents suffer and . . . sacrifice themselves voluntarily."[3]

It is hardly surprising that this widespread distress produced a demand for scapegoats. Politicians were accused of corruption and inadequate responses; corporate giants were excoriated for manipulating the crisis to their own profit. And the era's internationalist policies were blamed for making Japan vulnerable to other countries' problems. "The global economic crisis did more than any imperialist polemic," writes historian Tak Matsusaka, "to discredit the claims of the new diplomacy."[4] As a result, more and more

Fig. 6.1. One reason the Great Depression hit Japan's farms so hard was that nearly all farmers in the early 1930s still used the antiquated methods of this family, living in tightly packed villages and tilling their rice paddies by hand. Modernity did not come to Japan's farms until after World War II. (Courtesy of the U.S. National Archives.)

Fig. 6.2. Sagoya Tomeo, the twenty-three-year-old right-winger who attacked Prime Minister Hamaguchi Osachi in November 1930 in opposition to the London naval agreement, is held by officials at the Hibiya Police Station. The prime minister died the following August. (Nippon Dempo news service, courtesy of the U.S. National Archives.)

critics began demanding that Japan separate itself from the international system and develop a more aggressive foreign policy.

Event Two. The cries for more forceful diplomacy multiplied in 1930 after another episode heightened the impression that Westerners saw Japan as inferior. This crisis was precipitated by a London naval conference called to revisit the agreements made in Washington eight years earlier. The Japanese government went into the talks promising to insist on a 10-10-7 ratio for all cruisers, which would give Japan an additional 10 percent of the shipping tonnage maintained by Great Britain and the United States in that category, a level that experts agreed would enable Japan to control its surrounding waters. Negotiations continued from January through April, and in the end both sides compromised, agreeing to a 10-10-7 ratio on small cruisers and destroyers and complete parity in submarines but maintaining the 10-10-6 formula for large cruisers.

Japanese naval officials protested that 10-10-6 was not acceptable even for the large cruisers, and when prime minister Hamaguchi Osachi's cabinet ratified the treaty anyway, an uproar ensued. Many editorialists accused Hamaguchi of defying the military's "right of supreme command"; others decried an unequal international system and demanded that Japan begin to hew an independent course. On November 4, a young right-winger shot the prime minister at the Tokyo train station. On learning of the attack, which eventually took Hamaguchi's life, former Prime Minister Saionji Kinmochi commented, "When the public is treated to the spectacle of admirals and vice-admirals, and similar well-informed persons, issuing statements that 'the supreme command has been contemned' or that 'the London Treaty is against the nation's interest,' of course such statements are an incitement to young ignoramuses."[5] The calls for more aggressive diplomacy continued, however, not from "ignoramuses" but from an increasing number of elite opinion makers.

Event Three. A third crisis, which occurred a year later in Manchuria, turned indignation over the Great Depression and diplomacy into a conflagration. The voices demanding fuller control of Manchuria already had multiplied following Zhang Zuolin's 1928 assassination. In January 1931, a former Mantetsu official told the Diet that the government was doing nothing to counter anti-Japanese activities in China. And that same summer, after Chinese resisters attacked a settlement of two hundred Koreans who had immigrated to eastern Manchuria, settlers' organizations sent representatives to Tokyo to demand more military support. They received a tepid official response but heated public sympathy. Meanwhile, in Manchuria, several Japanese army officers decided that it was time to force the government to be more aggressive.

Ishiwara, the army college instructor, was in Manchuria now, determined to get his government to prepare for that "final war." Convinced that Japan was losing opportunities to take over Northeast China, he conspired with other officers to create an opportunity Tokyo could not ignore. On the night of September 18—while an official who had been sent to check on the radicals was asleep at a city restaurant, drunk—they set off an explosive on a section of the South Manchurian Railway just north of Shenyang (Mukden), making it look like the work of Chinese saboteurs. The damage was slight, but the impact of what came to be known as the Manchurian Incident was massive. The next day Japan's Guandong Army took control of the city, and three days later it sent troops northeast to the city of Jilin, where Ishiwara's group triggered incidents to make it appear that the 900 Japanese residents were in danger. Jilin, too, fell quickly. The Guandong Army also began removing Zhang Xueliang's 330,000-man army from the region. All the while, the cabinet was thrown into disarray, with most ministers irate over the insubordination yet convinced that they had no political choice but to publicly confirm the army's actions. They balanced their official approval with insistence that the army refrain from taking additional territory or raising taxes in the region.

Even the cabinet's restrictions were futile. Across the next months Guandong Army officials took repeated steps to turn Manchuria into an "independent" state. They appointed China's last Manchu emperor, Pu Yi, as a puppet executive, set up local governments under Japanese supervision, and the following February created Manchukuo—a state that officials privately described as "outwardly . . . under Chinese administration but actually under our control."[6] The most troubling feature of the process lay in the insubordination of the Guandong Army, abetted by expansionist bureaucrats back in Tokyo. Repeatedly, the government would resist aggressive new steps, then capitulate to actions on the field. And the Western powers, preoccupied with economic crises, responded as the activists had predicted—weakly. The United States refused to recognize Manchukuo, and the League of Nations spent a year investigating before adopting a February 1933 report that denied Japan's claim to have acted in self-defense and recommended the maintenance of both Chinese sovereignty and Japan's special interests. By then, events had moved to new levels.

If scheming military officers triggered Japan's aggression in Manchuria, the public response assured its continuation. Wearied by economic struggles and diplomatic compromises, citizens were eager for "positive" news. And the press gave them just that, with a torrent of enthusiastic articles following the Manchurian Incident. Films lauded each army move, lecturers toured the country praising the creation of Manchukuo, and radio stations broadcast live accounts of defense drills, military funerals, and troop send-offs. The few contrary editorialists who urged the government to restrain the army were drowned out in the public clamor. Depression had left the public anxious, and the London naval agreement had inspired new levels of paranoia. Now the Manchurian Incident stirred up public chauvinism. Internationalism, in short, had been overwhelmed by world events. And as a result, phrases such as "economic independence" and "glorious isolation" began to pepper public discussions.

7

SELF-SUFFICIENCY: THE ELUSIVE GOAL
(1932–1937)

Kiryū Yūyū was an irascible newspaper editor, as independent as he was incorruptible. When the widely admired general Nogi Maresuke captured the nation's imagination by committing ritual suicide after Emperor Meiji died in 1912, Kiryū called the act "meaningless." When the government conducted air raid drills over Tokyo in 1933, he scoffed that war would find Tokyo "reduced to ashes" and was forced to resign from his paper. Two years later he wrote a piece in his own private magazine, warning that if a "second world war" came it would be "more cruel, more inhuman, even than the first one." And in 1936, after a coup attempt by soldiers in Tokyo, he wrote that "the harm the military will do, if left unchecked, will be beyond imagining."[1]

Kiryū was not the only opponent of military expansion, but the sharp loneliness of his voice captured the changed nature of the 1930s. By the time of his "second world war" piece, liberal voices were heard more often in shadowy corners than on Main Street. Much of the country's activity now seemed to take its cue from what was happening in the expanding empire, where the creation of Manchukuo had betokened a new age. "Had Japan been content with the modest colonial empire which she had assembled by the end of World War I," writes Mark Peattie, "the course of history would have been profoundly different."[2] Instead the country's leaders had revised their fundamental goals; they sought now to weld the empire into a self-sufficient, or autarkic, unit that would assist Japan economically and assure Japan a permanent, significant place on the continent. Every aspect of life in the 1930s, both domestic and foreign, was shaped by that new goal.

The transformation was obvious across the empire. In Karafuto, which always had been administered directly from Tokyo, the residents (90 percent of them Japanese immigrants) were pushed to increase their output of wood, coal, and oil; they provided 70 percent of Japan's pulp across the 1930s. In Nan'yō, too, the focus shifted toward assisting in the drive toward autarky. The Micronesian economy thrived, thanks to the heavy demand for products such as sugar, phosphate, copra, and dried bonito, but the psychological costs of the new policies were high. *Assimilation* became a code word as colonial authorities used everything from schools to shrines to impose patriotism. The islands also were prepared for possible military activities, as officials gave increasing thought to Micronesia's strategic value. Although Japan generally observed League of Nations restrictions against arming the islands, officials launched large construction programs in the late 1930s, using thousands of immigrants (including two thousand Japanese prison inmates) to build communications facilities, airports, and naval bases with important offensive potential.

In Taiwan, the early 1930s saw a continuation of the previous decade's softer policies, with civilian governors-general reducing police control and allowing experiments in local self-government. The years also produced several Taiwanese cultural movements, which supported everything from women's rights to vernacular literature and Taiwanese suffrage. By mid-decade, however, the new expansionism had swamped most of these movements. As in Nan'yō, assimilation efforts (*kōminka*) resulted in the creation of mass organizations to inculcate Japanese values and the use of schools to create patriots. Even mountainous aboriginal peoples were pulled into these programs. After 1936, admirals and generals again filled the governor-general post. And economic development took center stage after 1935, when a Taipei conference on industrial expansion resulted in huge hydroelectric plants, improved harbors, and new aluminum factories, along with plants to process imported iron ore, rubber, and bauxite. By decade's end, Taiwan had become in the historian Hui-yu Caroline Tsai's words, a "disciplinarian society,"[3] an industrial engine for war.

Korea may have felt the post-Manchukuo priorities in the most intense way. On one hand, it lost its preeminence as the empire's central colony; Manchukuo had become the jewel. On the other hand, it became a more important development agent than ever, providing resources for Manchukuo's economic machine and turning Northeast Asia's rich natural resources into usable products.

The drive toward economic self-sufficiency had a two-sided impact on Korea. The result discussed most often was dark and heavy. Koreans hated the stepped-up effort to turn them into loyal subjects of the Shōwa Emperor, who had taken the throne in 1926. They were required to attend Shinto shrines after 1934, and school lessons turned more doctrinaire. The rural populations faced spreading poverty, too, as poor peasants continued losing land to more affluent farmers, both Japanese and Korean, who had connections to the colonial authorities; in 1936 more than three hundred thousand village families were reportedly using primitive slash-and-burn farming techniques to survive.[4] On the other hand, the cities experienced new cultural vitality, fueled by the expansion of factories as well as the growth of new media such as radio, movies, and commercial publishing (with phonograph records selling up to fifty thousand copies each). And the massive push toward industrialization brought prosperity to a number of new groups.

Determined to create an integrated, empirewide economy, Tokyo turned Korea into history's most heavily industrial colony. To guide the economy, the government provided low-interest loans to favored firms, arranging for financing primarily through the Korean Industrial Bank and the Bank of Chōsen. Those firms built highways and railroads, established textile factories and oil refineries, and constructed plants to produce explosives, chemicals, electricity, and iron, doubling the number of industrial workers in the 1930s to more than seven hundred thousand. While most entrepreneurs were Japanese, some were Korean. One Japanese, Noguchi Jun, built the world's second-largest dam and its second-largest chemical plant. A Korean, Kim Sŏngsu, developed the structures in these years that would turn the Kyŏngbang Spinning and Weaving Company into Korea's first multinational giant. Carter J. Eckert, a scholar of Korean capitalism, argues that Korea's post–World War II economic success was rooted in these years, in "a core of veteran businessmen, many of whom had been tempered . . . first and foremost in the rapid industrial growth of the late 1930s and early 1940s."[5]

On September 15, 1932, a year after the Manchurian Incident, Tokyo formally recognized Manchukuo under an agreement that put Japan in charge of the country's ports, railways, and airports and allowed the Guandong Army to place advisers in the government. Supposedly a sovereign country, Manchukuo had become a colony, an example of what Louise Young calls "autonomous imperialism."[6] Two developments underscored that fact. The first was the Guandong Army's victory over Mantetsu in taking charge of administrative affairs in Northeast China. The two had struggled after the Manchurian Incident, with Mantetsu officials (backed by the Foreign Ministry in Tokyo) trying unsuccessfully to curtail army expansionists. When Tokyo put Manchukuo under a Manchurian Affairs Board in 1934, presided over by the war minister, the Foreign Ministry was largely removed as a Manchurian actor and Mantetsu lost its preeminence. A December cabinet memo stating that Japan should "exploit internal strife in China to bring about a change in China's anti-Japan policy" demonstrated how fully the military thinkers had taken charge.[7]

Fig. 7.1. Japanese schoolgirls in Manchuria marched by the headquarters of the Guandong Army on September 18, 1933, to celebrate the second anniversary of the Manchurian Incident, which precipitated Japan's takeover of Northeast China. (Rengo news service, courtesy of the U.S. National Archives.)

The second crucial development, the country's growing isolation from the West, was dramatized on March 27, 1933, when Japan left the League of Nations. After the league accepted the investigatory Lytton Commission's conclusion that the Manchurian operations had been neither spontaneous nor defensive, Japan's representative to the league, Matsuoka Yōsuke, walked out, declaring that the Westerners were trying to "crucify" his land. "In a very few years," he said, "world opinion will be changed and . . . we also shall be understood by the world as Jesus of Nazareth was."[8] Other Japanese leaders put things more diplomatically and many questioned the wisdom of withdrawal, but there was no denying the new direction. After generations in which policy-making had been dominated by those who desired to succeed *within* the international system, the initiative had been seized by those who were determined that Japan should hew its own, autonomous path. As the future Prime Minister Konoe Fumimaro argued in a 1933 article defending the creation of Manchukuo, Japan had been forced to go it alone by imperialist powers bent on maintaining the status quo. The world, he thought, was divided between the powerful insider nations and those on the outside, which had to pursue their own interests or be overwhelmed. "They are in no position to judge us," he wrote of the former. "We had no choice but to advance into Manchuria and Mongolia. It was a matter of national survival."[9]

That meant that the country would have to find ways to protect itself against ever-new threats, perceived and real, for expansion breeds enemies—and a sense of vulnerability. One of the new worries was the Soviet Union, which responded to Japan's activities in Manchuria by enlarging its own army and air force in the east. Another was China, where Chiang Kaishek's control was growing stronger despite the Communist rebels' opposition. By the mid-1930s, hundreds of thousands of what the Japanese called "bandits"—former soldiers of Zhang Xueliang, local farmers, and Communist guerrillas—surrounded Manchukuo's population centers, engaging in everything from theft and petty violence to frontal attacks on Japanese-controlled villages and troops.

One response was to triple the size of the Guandong Army from fewer than sixty-five thousand in 1931 to two hundred thousand in 1937. Another was to take more territory. Korea was no longer a sufficient buffer zone; nor was Manchuria. Now Manchukuo needed its own "line of advantage." And so it would go. After attacks in China proper, Japan coerced Chiang Kaishek to sign the Tanggu Truce in May 1933, giving the Japanese control of the mountain passes east of Beijing and demilitarizing the area between Beijing and the Great Wall. For its part, Japan withdrew to the region north of the Great Wall but only temporarily. By early 1935, the Guandong Army had decided to create a regional government in North China, and the hawkish factions were calling for even further advances to protect new holdings and secure better ores and fuels. In December 1935, Chiang agreed to withdraw from the northern provinces of Hebei and Chahar and to place that region under a council largely controlled by Japan, another buffer zone that would need to be defended.

Meanwhile, the Japanese threw immense resources into developing Manchukuo. Convinced that Northeast China was the key to independence from the rest of the world, the government set up a Japan-Manchukuo Economic Bloc, with a shared currency, and created twenty-six new corporations under a plan to have one company per major industry. Tokyo poured nearly six billion yen into Manchukuo between 1932 and 1941, more than had been invested in the entire empire prior to this time. Japan built new railways and created nearly fifty new cities. Mantetsu became a massive research arm for the empire, with thousands of scholars studying colonial policy. And by the end of the decade more than three hundred thousand poor Japanese farmers had migrated to the region, supplementing the million Japanese living in Manchukuo's cities. They inhabited a thousand villages, providing crops for export and a human line of protection against Russian armies and Chinese resisters.

The homeland changed in the 1930s as much as the empire did. The transformation was not instantaneous, nor did it pervade all areas of life. Indeed, just as the 1920s had produced foreshadowings of militarism, the 1930s heard echoes of Taishō pluralism. People still crowded cafés as Japan's economy recovered, and the number of waitresses doubled between 1929 and 1936. Radio turned singers and baseball players into stars. Sixty-five thousand people turned out to watch Babe Ruth play in Tokyo in 1934, while theaters attracted throngs with "nonsense films." Elections continued, too, more often than not sending relatively liberal men to office. And contrarians such as Kiryū persisted in their shadowy corners. As late as 1937, after Japan launched wider hostilities in China, the Tokyo University professor Yanaihara Tadao could still lament in a public lecture that "the Japan . . . which we have loved so much . . . has lost its ideals."[10]

But each year saw a more militarized society. Nationalist organizations proliferated. On May 15, 1932, a group of right-wing naval officers masterminded the assassination of Prime Minister Inukai Tsuyoshi, who had angered them by attempting to check the army's activities in Manchuria. While they failed in their goal of triggering a military takeover of the government,

Fig. 7.2. All was not seriousness in the Japan of the mid-1930s, as evidenced by this 1936 contest for the country's longest, most beautiful beard. The winner was Naojirō Katō, age seventy-two, whose beard measured more than six feet. (Domei News, courtesy of the U.S. National Archives.)

their courtroom defense of patriotism encouraged a rise in nationalist rhetoric. One of the most widely read writers in these years was Kita Ikki, a national socialist who urged Japan to liberate Asia from Western control and called for a military coup to purify the government. Japan, he declared, was "the noble Greece of Asian culture," designed to "lift the virtuous banner of an Asian league and take the leadership in the world federation that must come."[11]

By mid-decade, the nationalistic mood was pervasive. Youth magazines displayed schoolchildren carrying rifles. Left-wing professors lost their jobs at national universities. Socialists announced their conversion to patriotism, often in an effort to avoid ostracism or prosecution. Several national figures were assassinated by ultranationalists. And people across the spectrum wrote about the hypocrisy of Western imperialists who criticized Japan's colonial moves while holding onto their own colonies. No one's experiences better illustrated the shifting tone than those of the political theorist Minobe Tatsukichi, a member of the Diet's upper house. When he publicly criticized the militaristic shift in 1934, and then refused the next spring to retract either the criticism or his theory that the emperor was just one (albeit a central one) of several organs of state, the right wing forced him out of office.

Fig. 7.3. Eleven army officers, convicted of assassinating Prime Minister Inukai Tsuyoshi on May 15, 1932, were sentenced here by a panel of judges to relatively short jail terms. Their passionate, nationalistic defenses during the trial inflamed the national mood. (World Wide Photos, courtesy of the U.S. National Archives.)

Reinforcing the new tone was the government's increasing authoritarianism, a development that resulted in part from the fragmented nature of cabinets under the carefully balanced Meiji constitutional system and the military's resultant success in manipulating the government. Political party leaders no longer served as prime ministers after Inukai's assassination; indeed, all but three of the eleven prime ministers from 1932 to 1945 were army or navy men. Officials also began to centralize the economy, coordinating policies with the *zaibatsu* (financial cartels) and the military. Electrical power was nationalized, a Cabinet Planning Bureau was created, and "discussion councils" were set up in factories to undercut labor activism. Elections continued, and the parties retained significant influence, but the movement toward Ishiwara's dream of a mobilized state was unmistakable.

Any doubts about the scope of the ultranationalists' goals vanished on the snowy morning of February 26, 1936, when fourteen hundred officers, mostly from the army's expansionist Imperial Way faction, attempted a coup, murdering three top officials and seizing central Tokyo. The government responded forcefully, moving forty ships into Tokyo Bay and mobilizing ten battalions, then, after speedy trials, executing the coup leaders (including Kita Ikki). But, while the strong response brought right-wing terrorism to an end, the incident initiated a shift in cabinet policies toward further cooperation with the military establishment. In August, the cabinet approved a list of contingencies that might make war in Asia necessary. And Tokyo moved farther from its old Western allies, letting the Washington and London naval agreements lapse and signing an Anti-Comintern Pact with Germany in November, agreeing to cooperate in preventing the spread of communism.

Back on the continent, Japanese troops took things into their own hands again in mid-1937, and Tokyo's response recalled the Manchurian Incident rather than the previous year's coup attempt. When soldiers on maneuvers near the Marco Polo Bridge outside Beijing heard shots from an unknown source on the night of July 7, they responded by attacking the local Chinese army. Hostilities ebbed and flowed over the next weeks, as diplomats struggled to contain the fighting while nationalists in both China and Japan made bellicose statements about the other side's "aggression." In a reprise of 1931, the cabinet came down finally, though reluctantly, on the side of the military, and by late July the two countries were at war. Said the diplomat Ishii Itarō, "The dog . . . once again, without its master's bidding, went mad in attacking another party."[12] The central imperialist motif of the 1930s—the drive for self-sufficiency—had pushed Japan farther and farther into China. Now it also had produced another war.

8

THE END OF EMPIRE
(1937–1945)

Takahashi Aiko, who lived in central Tokyo, complained in her diary eighteen months into the Pacific War, "Today, we had an air-defense drill again. The community council big shots put on their pompous clothes and their pompous faces and strutted about with a pompous number of people." On a Thursday during the following year, she wrote that radio announcers had described "victory" in a battle she was sure Japan had lost: "I couldn't help but feel contempt for the authorities who treat us as though we were stupid." And during the summer of 1945 she said that in the midst of "this hell of unremitting anxiety and sadness" she had discovered pleasure, for "swallows had built a nest on the light fixture . . . and were raising cute babies." Takahashi's diaries tell us unexpected things about wartime Japan. They describe a country in which daily life went on even as battles raged. They make it clear that people were well aware, quite early, that disaster was on the way. And they counter stereotypes of a blindly loyal citizenry. As she wrote after hearing about the atomic bombs on August 9, "I can't help but hate those responsible for placing human beings in this situation and continuing the war."[1]

Many reasons have been given for Japan's descent into World War II: the unstoppable pull of expansionism, once it was adopted as policy in the nineteenth century; the decision to move toward autarky after the Great Depression; the effectiveness of right-wing propaganda and the military's takeover of the government in the early 1930s; the diplomatic ineptitude of officials (both American and Japanese) in the late 1930s; the use of the imperial institution as a propaganda tool to inculcate nationalist loyalties; and the refusal of the Shōwa Emperor himself to make serious efforts to slow the march toward militarism. All of these played a role. But there was another cause at least as important—the web of imperialism. The imperialist mind-set, abetted by the colonial infrastructure that encircled Asia in the late 1930s, not only helped to propel Japan toward war but influenced nearly every action once the war had begun.

Fig. 8.1. As Japanese troops took control of central China in 1938, frightened villagers often greeted them with gifts as peace offerings. Here, in Jiangxi, the offering was a pig ready to be butchered. (World Wide Photos, courtesy of the U.S. National Archives.)

Ishiwara, the mastermind of the Manchurian Incident, warned against expansion into China in 1937. China was too big and complex, he argued; taking it on would be stepping into a morass. But the logic of imperialism trumped his counsel, and Japan soon found itself mired in China. Although Japanese troops won victories at Shanghai in November and Nanjing in December, before establishing formal control over most of coastal China the next year, the victories exacted a heavy toll. The Shanghai battle, expected to be relatively easy, consumed three full months, at a cost of 40,000 Japanese and 250,000 Chinese casualties. In Nanjing, military success was followed by one of the worst outrages in this, or any, war: a seven-week orgy of violence in which Japan's soldiers raped and murdered tens, probably hundreds, of thousands of civilians and fleeing soldiers. To this day, the Nanjing Massacre causes sharp tensions between China and Japan.

Meanwhile, Chiang Kaishek fought back by retreating, first to the Yangzi River city of Wuhan, then to Chongqing, west of the river's grand gorges. He also delayed Japan's advances in the north by dynamiting dikes on the Yellow River, a strategy that destroyed at least four thousand villages and outraged his own people as much as it stymied the Japanese. While Japan won many victories, the negatives were daunting: 70,000 troops killed by the end of 1937, 850,000 soldiers stewing in China by decade's end, and little prospect of victory once Chiang had ensconced himself in Chongqing. The Soviet Union added to the woes, first by supplying Chiang with money and arms and then, in the summer of 1939, by defeating Japan in a three-month clash in the arid Nomonhan region along Manchuria's border with Mongolia, a struggle that left nearly 18,000 Japanese dead.

Worst of all, arguably, was the war's psychological and moral toll. Many credit battlefield frustrations, along with racist attitudes, with inspiring an endless series of atrocities by Japan's military, acts that belied Japanese beliefs about their own spiritual superiority. The long-hushed human experiments of Manchuria's Unit 731 were particularly heinous, with soldiers injecting thousands of civilians with diseases such as typhoid and bubonic plague in an effort to develop military strategies. "I had already gotten to where I lacked pity," one unit member confessed after the war. He said that he and his fellows "had to struggle with our humanity afterward. . . . It was an agonizing process. There were some who killed themselves, unable to endure."[2]

Japan's officials struggled vainly for a coherent policy as the 1940s dawned. Their goal remained steady—victory over China—or, if that was not possible, assurance of permanent control of Manchukuo. The means to reach that goal became increasingly elusive, however. The army was bogged down in China. Russia threatened in the north. Resources were dwindling.

And then there were the Americans, who had begun countering Japan's offensive with financial and trade restrictions. In 1939, America abrogated the U.S.-Japan commercial treaty; the next year it restricted the sale of aviation gasoline and scrap iron, as well as iron and steel; by early 1941 it had embargoed most other metals; and in July 1941 it froze Japanese assets in the United States and stopped the sale of oil. Each move was regarded by Tokyo as economic warfare.

Japan's responses to these developments were largely ad hoc. In September 1940, Tokyo strengthened its ties with Germany and Italy, signing a Tripartite Pact that recognized their predominance in the West and Japan's in the East. In April 1941, a five-year neutrality pact with the Soviets secured the northern border. Then, in July, Japan expanded the military arena by moving troops into French-controlled southern Indochina (present-day Vietnam, Cambodia, and Laos), a region rich in the oil, rubber, and mineral resources that Japan needed. One result of these moves was the intensification of negotiations with the United States, with Japan determined to secure, at the very least, recognition of its holdings in Northeast China and the Americans insistent on removing Japan from China altogether. After the Americans refused repeatedly to compromise on either China proper or Manchuria, Prime Minister Tōjō Hideki made Tokyo's intentions clear at an imperial policy conference on December 1, 1941: "Some . . . would like to avoid war . . . but even these people have made up their minds that as long as the United States refuses to acknowledge our legitimate position, does not remove the economic blockade, and refuses to abandon her policy of oppressing Japan, our moving southward is inevitable; and if this action leads to a clash between Japan and the United States, this also cannot be helped."[3]

A week later, Japan was at war with the United States, having bombed Pearl Harbor in Honolulu on December 7. The wars in Europe and China had been joined in a global conflagration. The struggle's early months were heady for the Japanese. On the day on which they killed more than three thousand Americans in Honolulu, they also destroyed half of America's fleet in Manila and landed troops on the eastern coast of the Malay Peninsula. Over the next six months, they took nearly every target in the Pacific and Southeast Asia, with islands such as Guam and Wake falling in December and Hong Kong on Christmas day. Singapore fell in February, the Netherlands Indies in March, and the pivotal Philippines in May. "The violence, fury, skill, and might of Japan far exceeded anything we had been led to expect," said British Prime Minister Winston Churchill.[4]

The string of victories would not last, however. By the time it had taken the Philippines, Japan was engaged in a more difficult naval battle with the

Fig. 8.2. The Japanese attack at Pearl Harbor on December 7, 1941, destroyed more than half of America's Hawaiian fleet, including the destroyers *Downes* (left) and *Cassin*, and ignited war with the United States. The flagship of the Pacific Fleet, the *U.S.S. Pennsylvania* (rear), was only slightly damaged. (Courtesy of the U.S. National Archives.)

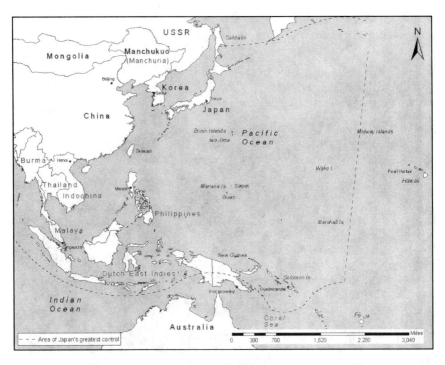

Map 3. Japan at War, 1937–1945. (Courtesy of Taylor Hafley.)

Allies at Port Moresby, off the southern coast of New Guinea, which ended in a stalemate but wiped out Japan's aura of invincibility. The next month, Japan suffered a major loss off Midway Island in the central Pacific after U.S. agents broke Japan's intelligence code. Then a lengthy battle in the south Pacific's Solomon Islands chain turned the war against Japan at Guadalcanal, a barren island of dense jungles and malaria-carrying mosquitoes. After losing 25,000 troops, 24 battleships, and 600 planes, Japan abandoned the island in January 1943. From that point on, Japan's efforts were largely defensive— and disastrous. On some Pacific islands, the casualties were horrific beyond telling; at Saipan, for example, almost 95 percent of Japan's 43,000 troops were killed and another 4,000 civilians committed mass suicide before the island fell in July 1944. By late that year, even the homeland was under attack by Allied bombers.

The war's central tale for this account lies in its impact on Japan's empire. The rhetoric actually became less imperialistic during the war, as Japanese officials claimed that they were creating a pan-Asian sphere of cooperating peoples in opposition to the old Western-style colonialism; they even made Karafuto into a prefecture in 1944. But the reality was harsher than ever. In 1938, Tokyo had begun talking about a New Order in East Asia, a system that would free the region from Western dominance. In 1940, the emphasis shifted to a Greater East Asia Co-prosperity Sphere, which included Southeast Asia as part of the growing economic regime. Now, engaged in the Greater East Asian War, colonial authorities threw their energy into making local populations support Japan's crusade with their resources as well as their loyalty.

The construction of airfields and naval bases was speeded up in Nan'yō, while authorities turned Taiwan into a staging area for continental military campaigns, intensifying assimilation programs and industrializing the island as never before. More than sixty thousand Taiwanese were inducted into Japan's armed forces and another two hundred thousand were recruited to provide supplemental tasks for the military. In Korea, mobilization and indoctrination reached every corner of society. By the early 1940s, schools no longer taught the Korean language, independent newspapers had been shut down, and families had been forced to take Japanese names. Even more devastating materially was the conscription of Koreans into the Japanese war effort, with as many as four million dispatched across the empire to serve in the military or in demeaning jobs. The worst victims were the one to two hundred thousand comfort women, most of them teenagers, forced to serve in war zone brothels. While women of many nationalities were coerced into this sex work, the vast majority were Koreans, many of whom suffered trauma long after the war was over. "When I returned home," recalled Yi Ki Bun, "I couldn't bear to hear mothers calling their children. I couldn't stand it, realizing I didn't have children and couldn't have any."[5]

If war brought mobilization to the old colonies, it introduced a variety of new colonial experiences to Southeast Asia, where the invading Japanese made different arrangements with different countries. Malaya and Indonesia came under direct military supervision, while Burma and the Philippines were given nominal autonomy under Japanese control. Thailand remained independent in return for allowing Japan to station troops and build prison camps there; Indochina continued as a colony of the German-Italian ally Vichy France; and tiny Portuguese Timor, north of Australia, remained a Portuguese territory but answered to the Japanese military. Regardless of the outward form, Tokyo dominated practically the entire region.

In justifying their rule, the Japanese talked sometimes about an *Asian* culture shared by members of a racial family and at other times—as at a 1943 Greater East Asia Conference in Tokyo—about *universal* ideals, such as "mutual cooperation," that would help the empire "construct an order of common prosperity and well-being based upon justice."[6] But none of the rhetoric masked Japan's determination to create pliant regimes that would assist in the war effort now and serve as building blocks in a Japanese world order later.

One feature of this wartime colonial order was hierarchical, racist thinking, which created lasting enmity throughout Southeast Asia. On the one hand, the Japanese saw themselves as superior. As the Pulitzer Prize–winning historian John Dower points out, nearly all Japanese were convinced now that the Japanese constituted "the 'leading race' of Asia and implicitly the whole world," a pure race destined to lead "the inferior peoples of Asia in an autarkic block."[7] Like colonists everywhere, most Japanese stereotyped their Southeast Asian subjects accordingly: always as inferior, usually as lazy, devious, or uncivilized. And their actions matched their prejudices. Living in their own lavish quarters filled with servants, colonial masters were notorious for slapping and beating subjects or showering them with verbal abuse. They changed local calendars to fit Japan's year-numbering system and coerced people to observe Japanese holidays. And they enforced laws arbitrarily. In Singapore, thousands of people accused of subversive activities were killed without fair trials, many of them reputedly by drowning. In Indonesia, "the rumor was that if the Kempeitai [military police] took you away, that was the end. You would not come back alive."[8] Perhaps a million Indonesians died under Japan's wartime policies, as did up to two hundred thousand Vietnamese whose rice paddies were converted into jute fields to meet Japan's war needs.

Another result of the wartime policies was the evisceration of many Southeast Asian economies. These nations had benefited from increased trade with Japan in the 1930s, but after 1941, as Japan reshaped them to serve its own needs, they suffered. In Indonesia and Thailand, Japan sought primarily food, in other countries oil, rubber, copper, bauxite, tungsten, tin, nickel, and manganese. Repeatedly, the result was negative, sometimes because of the disruption of traditional economic systems, sometimes because of Japan's deteriorating war situation. In the Philippines, for example, the forced conversion of sugar fields to cotton deprived farm families of food and income, just as the move to jute did in Vietnam. And Allied blockades and air raids on the region after 1944, combined with Japan's rapidly diminishing shipping capacity, made it difficult to transport even the goods that were produced, the result being that Japan imported less and less of the oil, rice, and iron ore that it was forcing Southeast Asians to produce. The colonies were thus left with goods that they could neither use at home nor sell abroad. The inability to construct viable economies in this region surely undercut Japan's overall war effort; it also devastated the Southeast Asian countries themselves.

The most unexpected effect of Japan's takeover was the undermining of the foundations of the Asian colonial structure, European and American as well as Japanese. The undoing began psychologically when colonial peoples saw European and American officials, men who had seemed so powerful and unassailable, humiliated by Japanese invaders in 1942. It continued with Japan's diatribes against Western imperialism, which, though hypocritical, energized anticolonial activists. Even more important was the training the Japanese provided to young men such as Burma's Aung San and Indonesia's Sukarno, who would lead postwar independence struggles, and the stimulation Japan's harsh measures gave to new resistance movements that, in their turn, would seize the arms of the Japanese and focus their wrath against Westerners at war's end. When Japan decided to surrender, a resistance group declared Indonesia free. And on September 2, 1945, the day of Japan's official surrender, Ho Chi Minh told half a million cheering supporters that Vietnam had become an independent state. These declarations would not keep the Westerners from returning later in 1945. But Japan's wartime activities changed the balance, and within a decade most Southeast Asian nations would throw off the colonial yoke.

Back in Japan, defeat was apparent everywhere by the summer of 1945. Allied planes were bombing the cities (thirteen million would be rendered homeless by August), and Okinawa fell on June 22 after the loss of as many as one hundred thousand Japanese troops and perhaps even more civilians. The domestic economy was in shambles, with many families living in makeshift huts and scrounging for food. And, with the war in Europe over, the Allies were concentrating on Japan. As the disasters multiplied, realists intensified their efforts to bring the war to an end. But hardliners insisted on continuing the fighting, and the Supreme War Council remained deadlocked throughout July, unable to agree on how, or even whether, to seek peace. When the Allied leaders issued an ultimatum from Potsdam in Germany on July 26, demanding that Japan surrender unconditionally or face destruction, the elderly Prime Minister, Suzuki Kantarō, responded with the word *mokusatsu*, a vague term that can mean either "to kill something with silence" or "to remain in wise and masterly inactivity." The Allies took this as a rejection.

Three events in early August finally pushed the war council into action. On August 6, the United States dropped the world's first atomic bomb on Hiroshima, turning that city into an incinerated hell and prompting President Harry Truman's warning of a coming "rain of ruin." Two days later, the Soviets voided their neutrality pact with Tokyo and entered the war against Japan. And on August 9 an atomic bomb hit Nagasaki. "The room was filled with a dazzling, brilliant light, as if a thousand magnesium flashes were

Fig. 8.3. The American assault on Okinawa in the spring of 1945 demolished the buildings and grounds of the old Shuri Castle, where kings once had ruled the Ryūkyū archipelago in splendor. Here U.S. troops look through the ruins. (*New York Times* photo, courtesy of the U.S. National Archives.)

ignited all at once," recalled a Nagasaki surgeon. And then, several hours later, "There were many corpses . . . burning. In the stream near the cathedral, there were the floating bodies of those who drowned when they jumped in fleeing from the unbearable heat and burns. Nevertheless, the night was calm and quiet, without any sound of human voices."[9] Together, the bombs killed more than two hundred thousand people, a third of the cities' combined population.

Some historians argue that the Soviet entry into the war affected Japan's leaders most sharply since it ended any chance for using Moscow as an agent in negotiating a face-saving end to the fighting. Others contend that the bombs were most important. In truth, it likely was the combined force of all three events that rendered the terminal blow, prompting the war council to accept the Potsdam Declaration on the provision that the emperor be spared. On August 15, the emperor—whose wartime responsibility has been debated ever since—spoke to the Japanese people in a scratchy radio recording; the time had come, he said, to surrender. "Tears ran down our cheeks," recounted the Tokyo diarist Yoshizawa Hisako on that day. "The streets were quiet. People's faces had no particular expression. Perhaps they were exhausted. As to how they felt about the war ending, an unmistakable brightness in their faces told the story."[10] The surrender ceremony occurred two and a half weeks later, on September 2, aboard the *U.S.S. Missouri*.

Following the Potsdam Declaration, the formal surrender document left no room for nuances on the issue of empire. Japan's military would be "completely disarmed," the Allies would occupy the country, and "Japanese sovereignty shall be limited to the islands of Honshu, Hokkaido, Kyushu, Shikoku and such minor islands as we determine."[11] In a single stroke, Japan had lost its colonies and with them its empire. Even the Ryūkyūs were gone, placed under American control in an arrangement that would last until Okinawa was returned to Japan in 1972. The buffer zone policy, which had pulled Japan ever farther afield, was dead. Defense would be assured now by a small Self Defense Force and a bilateral military arrangement with the Americans. Internationalism would once again, as in Meiji times, undergird national policy. And prosperity would depend on industry and trade rather than autarky or empire. "The harsh reality of 'defeat' is not an easy thing to stomach," wrote Yoshizawa six days after the emperor's announcement. "But the day probably will come when we see that . . . the results were not completely bad."[12]

CONCLUSION

J apan experienced more twists between 1850 and 1945 than a Kabuki script. Revolts succeeded, failed, and succeeded again. Commoner troops thrashed samurai battalions. Swords gave way to guns, which triumphed in their turn over Western armies. Modernity brought rickshaws to the streets, followed by cars and subways, while Confucian propriety withered before "modern girls" and movies. Afraid of being colonized, Japan developed an empire of its own, sending shopkeepers and officials off to Dalian, Taipei, and Pusan. And when it appeared that Japan had fulfilled its colonial dreams, it concocted more—during the very years when the Western powers had begun putting breaks on colonial development—and triggered a conflagration that incinerated the whole imperial enterprise. In all of this, Japan's experience with imperialism was both universal and unique, similar to the colonialism of the West yet imbued with its own distinctive qualities. Both the unique qualities and the universalities raised several issues with far-ranging implications.

One set of issues relates to causes. The American historian Walter Nugent has argued that "the significance of the frontier in American history . . . may well be that it instilled in Americans bad habits of building empires."[1] On the other side of the Pacific, it could be argued that the process of staving off Western imperialism infected the Japanese with an expansionist fever that could not be cured short of wartime defeat. It was Western imperialists who forced Japan into the global network of the mid-1800s. The scholar Yokoi Shōnan wrote in 1860 that China's humiliation by Western gunboats caused the Japanese "to shudder so that we cannot calmly sit back and watch" and then advocated strengthening Japan "economically and militarily in order to avoid indignities from other countries."[2] Most of the national agenda of the next thirty years was devised to meet that threat. Schools were built to create patriotic, literate citizens; the imperial institution was redefined to make it a source of both authority and patriotic loyalty; and industrialization was encouraged to confront Britain's economic juggernaut. Prime Minister Yamagata was thinking about the West's "new imperialism" when he called for a strong military to defend lines of sovereignty and advantage.

Each new step in national development from that point onward was influenced by the worldwide imperialist environment. As others have noted, capitalism had a limited impact on Japan's early colonial expansion; the motives were survival, power, and prestige. The late Meiji wars with China and Russia related fundamentally to the desire to secure Korea as a buffer against the Western powers. Even the later move into Manchuria was motivated partly by the need to establish a wall against Russia, which had poured so many resources into the area. Economic issues became important later, as Japan began to establish itself in its colonies, and these issues dominated after the Great Depression launched Japan on the road to autarky. But Japanese planners never stopped worrying about the threat of Western imperialism. The declaration of war following Pearl Harbor expressed the sincere concerns of most Japanese officials when it argued that "the trend of affairs would, if left unchecked, . . . endanger the very existence of Our nation." Fighting was justified as a struggle for "existence and self-defense."[3]

A second issue relates to the question of whether imperialism was the only path available to Japan. It was not. Many critics suggested alternative routes, particularly in the early twentieth century. The socialists used an internationalist vocabulary to oppose the Russo-Japanese War. Several years later the historian Asakawa Kan'ichi warned that expansionism was giving Japan a reputation as an "egotistic nation." And in the early 1920s, the economist (and later prime minister) Ishibashi Tanzan called colonies a liability. "I assert that giving up Greater Japanism will not be a disadvantage at all," he wrote. "If we give up lands like Korea, Taiwan, Sakhalin, and Manchuria and if we make vast China a friend, then . . . the whole Far East and all the weak and small countries of the world will become our moral supporters."[4] Others argued for more nuanced approaches, for the maintenance of Korea and Taiwan, for example, but greater caution in China. Critical voices eventually were overwhelmed by the cacophony of nationalism. But to the end, influential thinkers made it clear that Japan could have gone in quite different directions.

Still a third set of issues relates to the legacy of colonialism. Japan's experience with empire was briefer than most, lasting just fifty years. Greater Japan also differed in other respects from the Western empires: in its limited geographical expanse, in the homeland's cultural affinity with the colonies, in the unusually large number of administrators Japan sent to most regions, and in the strategic goals that drove it. And Japanese colonialism ended in unique fashion: quickly and involuntarily. How did all of these factors affect the colonies in the decades after the war?

There is little question, on the one hand, that colonialism produced many positive results. Educational levels rose in Korea, Taiwan, and Manchuria.

New infrastructures—railroads, factories, mines—remained for use by postwar governments, while industries that got their start under the Japanese became engines of economic growth later, particularly in Korea. Leadership nurtured during the Japanese years, sometimes as part of the colonial administration and sometimes as part of resistance movements, also shaped several countries in later years. And Japan's wartime activities undermined the foundations of the broader imperial structure. Even when locals loathed the Japanese, as they especially did in Korea, it was noteworthy, says Mark Peattie, that the "colonial presence served as both a goad and a model." He adds that "wounded . . . pride" made the Koreans doubly determined to succeed in later decades.[5]

None of these benefits washed away the enduring colonial stain, however: the humiliation of lost sovereignty, the propagation (and inculcation) of racist stereotypes, the expulsion of families from properties they had owned for generations, the psychological scars left by arrogant colonial administrators, the arrested and unequal development of local economies, the ripping apart of families, and the lasting debilitation of those whose health and reputations were destroyed in brothels, factories, and battlefields. The Tunisian Albert Memmi had Europeans in mind when he wrote, "Colonization materially kills the colonized. It must be added that it kills him spiritually. Colonization distorts relationships, destroys or petrifies institutions, and corrupts . . . both colonizers and colonized."[6] He could as well have been describing Japan's experience. Degradation was not the entire story, but it was an important part of it. And it would plague Japanese-Asian relations for generations to come.

A final issue springs from the way imperialism ended for Japan and its colonies. The Americans and Europeans typically *chose* to give independence to their colonies, sometimes under heavy pressure but nonetheless as a choice of their own. Japan, by contrast, had empire snatched away. Japan surrendered. War ended. The empire was gone. On the one hand, the abruptness of that process triggered postwar animosities. There was no winding down, no Japanese initiative, no time for reflection on reasons or modes for dismantling—one factor, certainly, in Japan's troubled experiences with its eastern Asian neighbors across the rest of the century. On the other hand, the dramatic nature of the demise enabled the Japanese to put the colonial episode aside quickly and focus on domestic development. The speed with which Japan reestablished a viable democratic system and recovered economically, creating the world's second-largest economy within a quarter of a century, has been heralded as a "miracle." And the completeness with which postwar Japan turned away from militarism has set it apart.

Japan's colonial history came to an end on September 2, 1945, when army chief Umezu Yoshijirō signed the formal surrender document aboard the battleship *U.S.S. Missouri*. Watching him were General Douglas MacArthur (left) and Lieutenant General Richard Sutherland. (*New York Times* photo, courtesy of the U.S. National Archives.)

Within a generation after the war, Japan had become a different kind of power, an economic giant with no desire to dominate others militarily (although some argued that imperialism had now taken on an economic garb). The totality of the loss in World War II was, by any reckoning, a major factor in shaping the Japan of the postwar years. With the empire crashing so quickly, a new reality took hold in the minds of most Japanese: the nectar of acquisition and allure of imperial power may be addictive, but they also are rife with peril and tragedy. Having experienced the bitterness of that reality directly, Japan's people would turn in a new direction in the second half of the twentieth century—a direction defined by trade and pacifism rather than empire and arms.

GLOSSARY

Autarky. Economic self-sufficiency; the policy that Japan pursued within its empire after the shocks of the Great Depression.

Chiang Kaishek (Jiang Jieshi). China's leader from 1928 until 1945. His weakness assisted Japan in moving into China in the 1920s and 1930s; he resisted firmly after 1937.

Colonialism. The policy of acquiring and controlling territories outside one's own sovereign borders.

Gotō Shinpei. One of Japan's most effective colonial administrators, first as head of civilian affairs in Taiwan, then after 1906 as director of the South Manchurian Railway Company. He became foreign minister in 1918.

Great Depression. Worldwide economic depression, which began in 1929 and rocked Japan's confidence in the international economic system, encouraging a move toward economic self-sufficiency and estrangement from the Western powers.

Guandong Army. Japan's Manchurian army, named after the Chinese region that it was created in 1906 to defend. It dominated Manchurian affairs in the 1930s.

Imperialism. One nation's assertion of control over another people, either by direct acquisition or by more informal means, usually economic, military, or political.

Ishiwara Kanji. Army college lecturer, and later a general, who advocated preparation for "total war" in the 1920s, masterminded the Manchurian Incident in 1931, and called for caution in China in 1937.

Karafuto. The southern half of the island of Sakhalin, which became a Japanese colony in 1905.

Liaodong. Peninsula at the southern end of Manchuria, taken by Japan in 1895 at the end of the Sino-Japanese War, given back to China after the Triple Intervention that year, then taken over by Japan again in 1905 after the Russo-Japanese War. It became the core of Japan's Manchurian colony.

Manchukuo. The puppet state formed by Japan in Northeast China in 1932 in the aftermath of the Manchurian Incident.

Manchuria. The name by which China's northeastern provinces were known. The southern part was developed by Japan after the Russo-Japanese War of 1904–05; after overrunning all of Manchuria in 1931, Japan turned the region into the puppet state of Manchukuo in 1932.

Manchurian Incident. Explosion set off near Shenyang on the South Manchurian Railway on September 18, 1931, which triggered Japan's takeover of Manchuria and led to the creation of the puppet state of Manchukuo.

March First Incident. Massive Korean uprising beginning on March 1, 1919, demanding independence from Japan; it galvanized nationalist sentiment and led to a decade of softer colonial policies.

Meiji. Reign name of the emperor from 1868 to 1912, when Japan underwent major modernization and initiated its imperialist policies.

Meiji Constitution. Asia's first national constitution, promulgated on February 11, 1889. It simultaneously made the emperor sovereign and expanded popular rights; its balancing of the power of different government branches created ambiguity, which allowed the military to become dominant in the 1930s.

Nationalism. A people's devotion to their nation's interests and culture; it can take both positive and negative forms.

New Imperialism. The rush of powerful nations in the late 1800s to take new colonies, mostly in Asia and Africa.

Russo-Japanese War. War between Russia and Japan, 1904–05, fought over conflicting interests in Manchuria and Korea. Japan's victory launched its imperial expansion on the Asian continent.

Ryūkyū Islands. Islands south of the Japanese archipelago, taken over by Japan in 1879 and named Okinawa prefecture.

Shinto. Japan's traditional religion, grounded in respect for the god-spirits (*kami*) in all natural beings, particularly for the personified dieties, ancestors, and natural objects that inspire awe. It was used to foster loyalty to Japan in the imperial colonies.

Shōwa (Hirohito). Emperor from 1926 to 1989. He presided nominally over World War II but was not brought before the Tokyo War Crimes Tribunal. The degree of his responsibility for the war still is hotly debated.

Sino-Japanese War. War between Japan and China, 1894–95, over rights in Korea, won by Japan. Taiwan, ceded by China at the end of the war, became Japan's first colony. The war initiated by Japan's invasion of China in 1937, which culminated in World War II, sometimes is referred to by this term too.

South Manchurian Railway Company (Mantetsu). Founded after the Russo-Japanese War, it oversaw the development of Japanese interests in Manchuria until superseded by the Guandong Army at the beginning of the 1930s.

Taishō. Emperor from 1912 to 1926, a time in which Japan's imperialist activities were less aggressive, though still strong.

Taiwan. Island off China's southeastern coast, which in 1895 became Japan's first colony.

Tokugawa. Family that ruled Japan from 1600 to 1868. It ended national seclusion policies in 1854 and began active engagement with the leading Western nations.

NOTES

INTRODUCTION

[1] J. A. Hobson, *Imperialism: A Study* (New York: Cosimo, 2005), 15.

[2] James C. Thomson Jr., Peter W. Stanley, and John Curtis Perry. *Sentimental Imperialists: The American Experience in East Asia* (New York: Harper Colophon, 1981), 310.

[3] Jürgen Osterhammel, *Colonialism: A Theoretical Overview* (Princeton: Marcus Wiener, 1997), 4.

[4] Frank Brinkley, *Japan Weekly Mail*, February 24, 1883.

[5] Y. Tak Matsusaka, "The Japanese Empire," in William M. Tsutsui, ed., *Companion to Japanese History* (Oxford: Blackwell, 2007), 235.

CHAPTER 1

[1] Fukuchi Gen'ichirō, *Kaiō jidan* (Recollections), Yanagida Izumi, ed., *Fuckuchi Ōchi shū* (Works of Fukuchi Ōchi). Vol 11 of *Meiji bungaku zenshū* (Collected works of Meiji literature). Tokyo: Chikuma Shobō, 1966, 293.

[2] Donald Keene, *The Japanese Discovery of Europe, 1720–1830* (Stanford: Stanford University Press, 1969), 109.

[3] S. Wells Williams, quoted in William L. Neumann, *America Encounters Japan: From Perry to MacArthur* (Baltimore: Johns Hopkins University Press, 1963), 40.

[4] Tōyama Shigeki, "Independence and Modernization in the Nineteenth Century," in Nagai Michio and Miguel Urrutia, eds., *Meiji Ishin: Restoration and Revolution* (Tokyo: United Nations University, 1985), 29.

[5] Entry for January 9, 1858, in Townsend Harris, *The Complete Journal of Townsend Harris* (Rutland, VT: Charles E. Tuttle, 1959), 496; Michael R. Auslin, *Negotiating with Imperialism* (Cambridge: Harvard University Press, 2004), 31.

CHAPTER 2

[1] *Tokyo Nichi Nichi Shimbun* editorial, translated in *Tokio Times*, February 24, 1877.

[2] Entry for April 28, 1868, in *The Diary of Kido Takayoshi*, trans. Sidney Devere Brown and Akiko Hirota (Tokyo: University of Tokyo Press, 1983), 1:5.

[3] Wm. Theodore de Bary, ed., *Sources of East Asian Tradition* (New York: Columbia University Press, 2008), 2:473.

[4] Roger F. Hackett, *Yamagata Aritomo in the Rise of Modern Japan, 1838–1922* (Cambridge: Harvard University Press, 1971), 116.

[5] Kayano Shigeru, *Our Land Was a Forest: An Ainu Memoir* (Boulder: Westview, 1980), 40–41.

[6] *Tokyo Nichi Nichi Shimbun*, May 13, 1874, in Matthew Fraleigh, "Japan's First War Reporter: Kishida Ginkō and the Taiwan Expedition," *Japanese Studies* 50, no. 2 (May 2010), 54.

[7] Bruce Cumings, *Korea's Place in the Sun: A Modern History* (New York: Norton, 2005), 102.

[8] David J. Lu, ed., *Japan, A Documentary History* (Armonk, NY: M. E. Sharpe, 1997), 353.

CHAPTER 3

[1] Jay Rubin, *Injurious to Public Morals: Writers and the Meiji State* (Seattle: University of Washington Press, 1984), 56.

[2] *Nihon*, February 11, 1889, in Yamamoto Taketoshi, *Shimbun to minshū* (Newspapers and the Masses) (Tokyo: Kinokuniya, 1973), 87. The rescript is reproduced in Marius B. Jansen, *The Making of Modern Japan* (Princeton: Princeton University Press, 2000), 411. America's Pledge of Allegiance was first used in schools two years later in 1892.

[3] Nakae Chōmin, *A Discourse by Three Drunkards on Government* (New York: Weatherhill, 1984), 115. Shigetaka is quoted in Kenneth B. Pyle, *The New Generation in Meiji Japan* (Stanford: Stanford University Press, 1969), 158.

[4] August 14, 1894, in Stewart Lone, *Japan's First Modern War* (London: St. Martin's, 1994), 29.

[5] Matsubara Iwagorō, *Saiankoku no Tōkyō* (Darkest Tokyo) (Tokyo: Shūeisha, Iwanami Shoten, 1988), 64.

[6] Leo Ching, *Becoming "Japanese": Colonial Taiwan and the Politics of Identity Formation* (Berkeley: University of California Press, 2001), 17.

[7] Shumpei Okamoto, *The Japanese Oligarchy and the Russo-Japanese War* (New York: Columbia University Press, 1970), 173.

[8] Steven Ericson and Allen Hockley, eds., *The Treaty of Portsmouth and Its Legacies* (Hanover, NH: Dartmouth College Press, 2008), 109–10.

CHAPTER 4

[1] Kaneko Fumiko, *The Prison Memoirs of a Japanese Woman* (Armonk, NY: East Gate, 1991), 75.

[2] Oka Yoshitake, "Generational Conflict after the Russo-Japanese War," in Tetsuo Najita and J. Victor Koschmann, eds., *Conflict in Modern Japanese History* (Princeton: Princeton University Press, 1982), 197.

[3] Ukita Kazutami, "The Future of South America and our Emigration Policy," *Taiyō* 16, no. 8 (June 1910): 4.

[4] *New York Tribune,* July 26, 1907; quoted in Alexis Dudden, *Japan's Colonization of Korea* (Honolulu: University of Hawai'i Press, 2005), 16.

[5] Raymond A. Esthus, *Theodore Roosevelt and Japan* (Seattle: University of Washington Press, 1967), 307.

[6] Mark Peattie, *Nan'yō: The Rise and Fall of the Japanese in Micronesia* (Honolulu: University of Hawai'i Press, 1988), 68.

[7] Cumings, *Korea's Place in the Sun,* 148.

[8] Michael E. Robinson, *Korea's Twentieth-Century Odyssey: A Short History* (Honolulu: University of Hawai'i Press, 2007), 47.

CHAPTER 5

[1] Junichirō Tanizaki, *Naomi* (San Francisco: North Point, 1990), 175.

[2] Miriam Silverberg, "The Modern Girl as Militant," in Gail Bernstein, ed., *Recreating Japanese Women, 1600–1945* (Berkeley: University of California Press, 1991), 250.

[3] John F. Howes, ed., *Nitobe Inazō: Japan's Bridge Across the Pacific* (Boulder: Westview, 1995), 261.

[4] Mantetsu is a contraction of the Japanese name for the railway, Minami Manshū Tetsudō.

[5] K. K. Kawakami, *Manchoukuo: Child of Conflict* (New York: Macmillan, 1933), 258.

[6] For Tanaka in 1916, see Frederick R. Dickinson, *War and National Reinvention: Japan in the Great War, 1914–1919* (Cambridge: Harvard University Asia Center, 1999), 117. For Shidehara in 1930, see de Bary, *Sources of East Asian Tradition,* 2:570.

CHAPTER 6

[1] Mark Peattie, *Ishiwara Kanji and Japan's Confrontation with the West* (Princeton: Princeton University Press, 1975), 57, 74.

[2] Michael A. Barnhart, *Japan Prepares for Total War: The Search for Economic Security, 1919–1941* (Ithaca: Cornell University Press, 1987), 18.

[3] Mikiso Hane, *Peasants, Rebels, and Outcastes: The Underside of Modern Japan* (New York: Pantheon, 1982), 115.

[4] Yoshihisa Tak Matsusaka, *The Making of Japanese Manchuria, 1904–1932* (Cambridge: Harvard University Asia Center, 2001), 379–80.

[5] Harada Kumao, *Fragile Victory: Saionji-Harada Memoirs* (Detroit: Wayne State University Press, 1968), 275–76.

[6] William G. Beasley, *Japanese Imperialism, 1895–1945* (Oxford: Clarendon, 1987), 194.

CHAPTER 7

[1] On Nogi's death, see Herbert Bix, *Hirohito and the Making of Modern Japan* (New York: HarperCollins, 2000), 43. On air raid drills, see William de Lange, *A History of Japanese Journalism* (Surrey, U.K.: Japan Library, 1998), 145. On world war and the coup attempt, see Ōta Masao, *Kiryū Yūyū* (Tokyo: Kinokuniya, 1972), 171–72, 174, respectively.

[2] Ramon H. Myers and Mark R. Peattie, eds., *The Japanese Colonial Empire, 1895–1945* (Princeton: Princeton University Press, 1984), 22.

[3] Hui-yu Caroline Tsai, *Taiwan in Japan's Empire Building* (London: Routledge, 2009), 162.

[4] Robinson, *Korea's Twentieth-Century Odyssey,* 83.

[5] Carter J. Eckert, *Offspring of Empire: The Koch'ang Kims and the Colonial Origins of Korean Capitalism* (Seattle: University of Washington Press, 1991), 254.

[6] Louise Young, *Japan's Total Empire: Manchuria and the Culture of Wartime Imperialism* (Berkeley: University of California Press, 1998), 47–52.

[7] James Morley, ed., *The China Quagmire: Japan's Expansion on the Asian Continent, 1933–1941* (New York: Columbia University Press, 1983), 90.

[8] Young, *Japan's Total Empire*, 154.

[9] Yoshitake Oka, *Konoe Fumimaro: A Political Biography* (Tokyo: University of Tokyo Press, 1983), 28.

[10] Nobuya Bamba and John Howes, eds., *Pacifism in Japan* (Kyoto: Minerva, 1978), 214.

[11] Wm. Theodore de Bary, Carol Gluck, and Arthur E. Tiedemann, comps., *Sources of Japanese Tradition*, 2nd ed., vol. 2, pt. 2 (New York: Columbia University Press, 2006), 273.

[12] Barbara J. Brooks, *Japan's Imperial Diplomacy: Consuls, Treaty Ports, and War in China, 1894–1938* (Honolulu: University of Hawai'i Press, 2000), 184.

CHAPTER 8

[1] Samuel Hideo Yamashita, *Leaves from an Autumn of Emergencies* (Honolulu: University of Hawai'i Press, 2005), 168 (entry for March 27, 1943), 176 (October 19, 1944), 185 (July 11, 1945), 187 (August 9, 1945).

[2] Tamura Yoshio, quoted in Haruko Cook and Theodore Cook, *Japan at War: An Oral History* (New York: New Press, 1992), 164.

[3] Nobutaka Ike, ed., *Japan's Decision for War: Records of the 1941 Policy Conferences* (Stanford: Stanford University Press, 1967), 272–73.

[4] Peter Duus, ed., *The Cambridge History of Japan,* vol. 6: *The Twentieth Century* (Cambridge: Cambridge University Press, 1988), 348.

[5] George Hicks, *The Comfort Women* (New York: Norton, 1995), 204.

[6] Joyce C. Lebra, ed., *Japan's Greater East Asia Co-prosperity Sphere in World War II: Selected Readings and Documents* (London: Oxford University Press, 1975), 93.

[7] John Dower, *War without Mercy: Race and Power in the Pacific War* (New York: Pantheon, 1986), 264–65.

[8] Saburō Ienaga, *The Pacific War, 1931–1945* (New York: Pantheon, 1978), 178.

[9] Martin Kawano, *The Cloud and the Light: Memories of a Japanese Christian Surgeon from Nagasaki* (Notre Dame, IN: Cross Roads Books, 1997), 2, 6. Kawano refers to Urakami Catholic Cathedral, which was located near the hypocenter of the blast.

[10] Yoshizawa Hisako, August 15, 1945, quoted in Yamashita, *Leaves from an Autumn of Emergencies,* 217.

[11] Robert J. C. Butow, *Japan's Decision to Surrender* (Stanford: Stanford University Press, 1954), 243.

[12] Yoshizawa Hisako, August 21, 1945, quoted in Yamashita, *Leaves from an Autumn of Emergencies,* 220.

CONCLUSION

[1] Walter Nugent, *Habits of Empire: A History of American Expansion* (New York: Knopf, 2008), 316.

[2] de Bary et al., comps., *Sources of Japanese Tradition,* 2nd ed., vol. 2, pt. 2, 189.

[3] *Communiques Issued by the Imperial General Headquarters (Since the Outbreak of the Greater East Asian War)* (Tokyo: Mainichi, 1943), front matter.

[4] For Asakawa, see Ken'ichi Goto, *Tensions of Empire: Japan and Southeast Asia in the Colonial and Postcolonial World* (Athens: Ohio University Press, 2003), 12. For Ishibashi, see de Bary et al., comps., *Sources of Japanese Tradition,* 2nd ed., vol. 2, pt. 2 (New York: Columbia University Press, 2006), 189.

[5] Duus, ed., *The Cambridge History of Japan,* 6:269.

[6] Albert Memmi, *The Colonizer and the Colonized* (Boston: Beacon, 1991), 151.

Suggestions for
Further Reading

Auslin, Michael R. *Negotiating with Imperialism*. Cambridge: Harvard University Press, 2004.

Barnhart, Michael A. *Japan Prepares for Total War: The Search for Economic Security, 1919–1941*. Ithaca: Cornell University Press, 1987.

Beasley, William G. *Japanese Imperialism, 1895–1945*. Oxford: Clarendon, 1987.

Boyle, John Hunter. *Modern Japan: The American Nexus*. New York: Harcourt Brace Jovanovich, 1993.

Brooks, Barbara J. *Japan's Imperial Diplomacy: Consuls, Treaty Ports, and War in China, 1894–1938*. Honolulu: University of Hawai'i Press, 2000.

Caprio, Mark. *Japanese Assimilation Policies in Colonial Korea, 1910–1945*. Seattle: University of Washington Press, 2009.

Cook, Haruko, and Theodore Cook. *Japan at War: An Oral History*. New York: New Press, 1992.

Cumings, Bruce. *Korea's Place in the Sun: A Modern History*. New York: Norton, 2005.

Dower, John. *War without Mercy: Race and Power in the Pacific War*. New York: Pantheon, 1986.

Dudden, Alexis. *Japan's Colonization of Korea*. Honolulu: University of Hawai'i Press, 2005.

Duus, Peter. *The Abacus and the Sword: The Japanese Penetration of Korea, 1895–1910*. Berkeley: University of California Press, 1995.

————. *The Japanese Discovery of America: A Brief History with Documents*. Boston: Bedford, 1997.

Duus, Peter, Ramon H. Myers, and Mark R. Peattie, eds. *The Japanese Informal Empire in China, 1895–1937*. Princeton: Princeton University Press, 1989.

————. *The Japanese Wartime Empire, 1931–1945*. Princeton: Princeton University Press, 1996.

Esselstrom, Erik. *Crossing Empire's Edge: Foreign Ministry Police and Japanese Expansionism in Northeast Asia*. Honolulu: University of Hawaii Press, 2009.

Fogel, Joshua A., ed. *The Nanjing Massacre in History and Historiography*. Berkeley: University of California Press, 2000.

Goto Ken'ichi. *Tensions of Empire: Japan and Southeast Asia in the Colonial and Postcolonial World*. Athens: Ohio University Press, 2003.

Hicks, George. *The Comfort Women*. New York: Norton, 1995.

Ienaga, Saburō. *The Pacific War, 1931–1945*. New York: Pantheon, 1978.

Iriye, Akira. *After Imperialism: The Search for a New Order in the Far East, 1921–1931*. New York: Atheneum, 1978.

Kerr, George H. *Okinawa: The History of an Island People*. Rev. ed. Rutland, VT: Tuttle, 1958.

Lebra, Joyce C., ed. *Japan's Greater East Asia Co–prosperity Sphere in World War II: Selected Readings and Documents*. London: Oxford University Press, 1975.

Matsusaka, Yoshihisa Tak. *The Making of Japanese Manchuria, 1904–1932*. Cambridge: Harvard University Asia Center, 2001.

McClain, James L. *Japan: A Modern History*. New York: Norton, 2002.

Mutsu Munemitsu. *Kenkenroku: A Diplomatic Record of the Sino-Japanese War, 1894–95*. Tokyo: University of Tokyo Press, 1982.

Myers, Ramon H., and Mark R. Peattie, eds. *The Japanese Colonial Empire, 1895–1945*. Princeton: Princeton University Press, 1984.

Peattie, Mark. *Ishiwara Kanji and Japan's Confrontation with the West*. Princeton: Princeton University Press, 1975.

_____. *Nan'yō: The Rise and Fall of the Japanese in Micronesia*. Honolulu: University of Hawai'i Press, 1988.

Robinson, Michael E. *Korea's Twentieth-Century Odyssey: A Short History*. Honolulu: University of Hawai'i Press, 2007.

Rubinstein, Murray A., ed. *Taiwan: A New History*. Armonk, NY: M. E. Sharpe, 1999.

Ruoff, Kenneth. *Imperial Japan at Its Zenith: The Wartime Celebration of the Empire's 2,600th Anniversary*. Ithaca: Cornell University Press, 2010.

Tsai, Hui-yu Caroline. *Taiwan in Japan's Empire Building*. London: Routledge, 2009.

Weiner, Michael. *Race and Migration in Imperial Japan*. New York: Routledge, 1994.

Yamashita, Samuel Hideo. *Leaves from an Autumn of Emergencies*. Honolulu: University of Hawai'i Press, 2005.

Yang, Daqing. *Technology of Empire: Telecommunications and Japanese Imperialism, 1930–1945*. Cambridge, Mass.: Harvard University Press, 2003.

Young, Louise. *Japan's Total Empire: Manchuria and the Culture of Wartime Imperialism*. Berkeley: University of California Press, 1998.